# FACE R
## *a beginner's guide*

J.M. Sertori

Hodder & Stoughton

A MEMBER OF THE HODDER HEADLINE GROUP

For Andrew Deacon

# About the Author

J.M. Sertori is the author of *The Little Book of Feng Shui, Feng Shui Hour-by-Hour* and the co-author of *Practical Paganism*.

Orders: please contact Bookpoint Ltd, 39 Milton Park, Abingdon, Oxon OX14 4TD. Telephone: (44) 01235 400414, Fax: (44) 01235 400454. Lines are open from 9.00–6.00, Monday to Saturday, with a 24-hour message answering service. Email address: orders@bookpoint.co.uk

*British Library Cataloguing in Publication Data*
A catalogue record for this title is available from The British Library

ISBN 0 340 77228 X

First published 2000
Impression number  10 9 8 7 6 5 4 3 2 1
Year                        2005 2004 2003 2002 2001 2000

Copyright © 2000 J.M. Sertori

All rights reserved. No part of this publication may be reproduced or transmitted in any form or by any means, electronic or mechanical, including photocopy, recording, or any information storage and retrieval system, without permission in writing from the publisher or under licence from the Copyright Licensing Agency Limited. Further details of such licences (for reprographic reproduction) may be obtained from the Copyright Licensing Agency Limited, of 90 Tottenham Court Road, London, W1P 9HE.

Illustrations by Claire Foley.

Typeset by Transet Limited, Coventry, England.
Printed in Great Britain for Hodder & Stoughton Educational, a division of Hodder Headline plc, 338 Euston Road, London NW1 3BH by Cox and Wyman Limited, Reading, Berks.

# CONTENTS

### Chapter 1 An introduction to face reading ............ 1

| | |
|---|---|
| The history of face reading | 2 |
| Simple features | 3 |
| How face reading works | 4 |
| The aim of this book | 5 |
| Looking at the face | 5 |

### Chapter 2 Elements and colours ............ 7

| | |
|---|---|
| The Fire element | 9 |
| The Water element | 9 |
| The Wood element | 10 |
| The Metal element | 11 |
| The Earth element | 12 |
| The interaction of the elements | 12 |
| Case study | 14 |

### Chapter 3 Major single features ............ 15

| | |
|---|---|
| The nose | 15 |
| Case study | 19 |
| The mouth | 19 |
| Teeth | 23 |
| Case study | 26 |

## Chapter 4  Double features                27

| | |
|---|---|
| The ears | 27 |
| Case study | 33 |
| The eyes | 34 |
| Case study | 43 |
| The eyebrows | 43 |
| Case study | 51 |

## Chapter 5  Cheeks, jaw and chin          52

| | |
|---|---|
| Cheeks | 52 |
| Jaw | 53 |
| Chin | 56 |
| Case study | 59 |

## Chapter 6  Yin and Yang                  60

| | |
|---|---|
| Yin and Yang | 60 |
| Yin aspects | 61 |
| Case study | 62 |
| Yang aspects | 62 |
| Case study | 62 |

## Chapter 7  Transient features            63

| | |
|---|---|
| The Mark of Worry | 64 |
| The Mark of Intellect | 64 |
| The Mark of Travel | 65 |
| The Mark of the 'Third Eye' | 66 |
| The Mark of Tears | 66 |
| The Mark of Power | 67 |
| The Mark of Friendship | 67 |
| The Mark of Prosperity | 68 |
| The Mark of Family | 69 |
| The Mark of Sensuality | 70 |
| The Mark of Diplomacy | 71 |
| Freckles and spots | 72 |
| Laughter lines | 73 |
| Case study | 74 |

**CONTENTS**

| | | |
|---|---|---|
| **Chapter 8** | **To the hairline and beyond** | **75** |
| | Double and triple lines | 75 |
| | Diagonal forehead lines | 76 |
| | Hair | 76 |
| | Case study | 78 |
| **Chapter 9** | **Precision readings** | **79** |
| | Palaces of Fortune | 79 |
| | Facial division by year | 80 |
| | Case study | 81 |
| **Chapter 10** | **Basic charts** | **82** |
| **Further Reading** | | **90** |

# AN INTRODUCTION TO FACE READING

*T*his book charts the Chinese art of face reading (Mian Xiang, but more normally Ming Xiang). With roots deep in traditional Chinese medicine, and elements of Taoism and divination, this ancient method of fortune-telling uses the shape and features of the face to determine one's character and fate. Ming Xiang does not mean literally 'face reading', but 'consultation on fate', because in Chinese thought, the face is just as much an indicator of future events and tendencies as the palm is in Western mysteries.

'Face' means a lot in the Far East. The mask one turns to the outside world is a central indicator of one's character. Since ancient times, Chinese sorcerers have perfected a way of seeing behind the mask to one's true face, and using the features one presents to the world to tell fortunes and see souls. Ming Xiang is not only about personality; in Chinese thought it is also inextricably linked to medical diagnosis. The features of the face can reveal symptoms of ill health and potential trouble, just as they can reveal the aspects of a person's personality.

Like feng shui, face reading is a collection of superstitions and observations. Parts of it are rooted in Chinese folklore, but other sections have a sound grounding in what we would nowadays call social sciences. Body language, non-verbal communication and psychology all contribute greatly to face reading, though in these modern times it is often written off as an idle pastime.

# The history of face reading

Many aspects of China's ancient thought are known to us today. The *I Ching* is still used to tell fortunes, feng shui is still used to harmonize living arrangements and tai qu (t'ai chi) is still used to harmonize the body. Face reading is part of the same general worldview.

Chinese philosophy recognizes that all things seek harmony and balance, the yin and yang of popular knowledge. It also recognizes that the universe is composed of five elements, and that these exert a particular influence on a person, depending on the particular concentrations of that element they may have.

In ancient China, face reading was just one of the skills employed by soothsayers, along with divination and astrology. Employees would have their fortunes read as guides to their character and suitability, and this would often include a study of their faces. Certain kinds of faces were thought to predispose people to certain kinds of occupation and behaviour, and if, to coin a phrase, someone's face fitted, they could be whisked up the promotional ladder. Most famously, the Qin Emperor demanded that all his portraits display his face with all the features in their proper proportion, whether or not it was a true likeness!

While this may sound strange to us today, our own culture is little different. A man who wears spectacles is not necessarily going to be bad at sports, but the chances are relatively high that he may be too short-sighted to participate actively. This is an example of a snap judgement we might make based on a single piece of evidence (the spectacles), but for a face reader it would be the starting point of a much deeper examination. The chances are also high that the subject reads more books, and that the intellectual look of the spectacles has actually bred an intellectual demeanour. Likewise, if someone chooses to wear contact lenses they do so for a reason. If it is not vanity, then it could be the adverse affect that spectacles have on an active life – the presence or absence of spectacles telling us all these things about a subject, not because of what they are, but because of the tiny effect we can reasonably expect them to exert on other aspects of their personality. Our ability to breathe, the way our teeth affect our ability to smile, or the position of our ears, all these things can exert slight influences on the way we live our lives.

Psychological profiling is not unknown for job applicants in our culture, but perhaps we are also using our own forms of face reading more often than we think. Why does the dentist put braces on crooked teeth? Why does the actress have her face altered surgically? What is this nebulous 'ideal' to which we are aspiring? In many ways, face reading presents a better alternative. Instead of pointing to one perfect form, it lists many differing kinds, and shows how different features interact in different ways.

Many critics of face reading claim it is little removed from phrenology, the discredited 'science' of anthropometrics. This Victorian belief held that one's character (be it criminal or saintly) was fixed in the bones of the skull. But one's facial fortune is not incontrovertibly embedded in the skull. It is in a constant state of flux, in tune with one's pallor and skin condition. Moles, spots, scars and blemishes come and go, and each has a subtle influence on your fortune. Face reading can point out predispositions and likely behaviour, but no person's reading can be set in stone because no person's face is ever constant. Changes in weight and general health will alter fortunes with each passing day – phrenology only allows for immutable generalities.

# Simple Features

There are many facets to face reading that require some practice. In the early stages, it is best to concentrate on the major features of the face – the eyes, nose, mouth and ears. There are several different types of each, and with a little effort, you will soon be noticing the various shapes and patterns. With the major features, it is simple to spot the difference, for example, between a down-turned or up-turned nose, or blue and brown eyes.

Other aspects of face reading are a little more difficult, but you should not be deterred. Reading the bones under the skin, for example, is not something you can do as a casual observer, and is best left until you have mastered the easy stages. The same applies to the face's many minor features – the distinctive spots, dots and blemishes that allow for a detailed reading. It is these that really make the difference between a true reading and a vague set of guesses (think of the difference between a newspaper astrology column and a personal consultation).

One other important point, which cannot be stressed enough – face reading is the study and appraisal of the *entire* face, not of isolated features. Don't be tempted to leap to conclusions about yourself or others until you have mastered the whole of this book. The basic building blocks of face reading are found in the chapters that follow, but the fine-tuning that gives a really in-depth reading can only be found in the interaction of the different parts of the face. Practise by all means in the early stages, but do not be too quick to judge – you may find that each successive chapter throws new light on the one before.

# How face reading works

As you learn the properties of a new set of features, the number of potential combinations rises exponentially. Experienced face readers can reel off a string of observations without apparent pause for thought, but while you are learning, it is a good idea to write down each of your readings. A reading of a single feature will usually present you with a single piece of information about your subject. Perhaps they are kind, indecisive or unapproachable. Each extra feature you check adds another variable into the mix. Sometimes your initial theories will be crowded out by overwhelming evidence to the contrary. More often than not, you will find that the first words you write down are duplicated by other features. Merely by looking at the collection of words you amass, you will be able to draw several conclusions.

# The aim of this book

Face reading in its entirety can be incredibly detailed. This book aims to introduce the simpler sets of readings in a gradual manner, moving to more detailed charts and almanacs for more fine-tuned face reading at the end.

It is my belief that face reading is much easier to understand when we can see the underlying reasoning – somewhere in the distant past of ancient Chinese thought are rooted genuine observations of character, and if we go back to these, they not only make more sense, but are far easier to remember. This book often explains the origins of these beliefs. Instead of merely throwing rules and regulations at the reader, it delves into the reasons behind the readings, often showing glimpses of a human science that predates psychology. Much of the lore of face reading is simplified through straightforward animal and object analogies. The book aims to employ a matter-of-fact approach, streamlining the necessary information and helping the fledgling face reader to remember both the name and shape of the feature using appropriate terminology.

The face is a mask turned to the outside world, and we are all actors in our daily lives. Much face reading is about seeing the tiny, almost imperceptible roots of a theatrical gesture before a person makes it. Biting one's lip, scowling in frustration or bursting into floods of tears can all be seen on the face. The trick is being able to tell when someone is crying inside before they start crying outside. Although obscured by centuries of superstition, many aspects of Chinese folklore are rooted in scientific fact. The book also provides the reader with regular exercises to help define their knowledge so far.

# Looking at the face

## Lighting

Natural light is the best, because apparent colour can be altered by the local light source. Tinted light bulbs, the ambient hue of a room caused by the reflection of paint from the walls, and even bleaching of colours caused by overly-bright lights, can all effect the precision of your readings. Since all these laws were originally formulated in comfortable, naturally lit surroundings, those are the best for you to duplicate. If, for some reason, you find yourself forced to perform a reading under adverse lighting conditions, remember to adjust your idea of colour accordingly.

## Test subjects

In the early stages, the only face you look at is likely to be your own. This is inadvisable – you may not like what you see, and may try and skew your ideas of certain kinds of readings to reflect yourself in a positive light. You may also be tempted to perform readings on your own family, but it is important to get some sort of variation. Variations within a family are likely to be much finer than between two unrelated members of the public, and the reading may involve making the kind of distinction that will only come after a little practice. Instead, try looking at strangers on the street, or pictures in magazines.

The best kind of face reading, and the most revealing, is fully interactive, in which you can quiz your subject, talk to them about the various things you are digging up, and perhaps feel for the shape of the bones underneath the skin (however, this is something to leave for when you have mastered the basics).

## This is face reading

One final and rather obvious point. This is a book about face reading. If you can't find a mirror and decide that when analysing general skin colour it is sufficient to look at your hands instead, you may be fooling yourself. Your hands may well be a slightly different hue to your face, and you can't judge by that. Remember – look at the face and the face alone.

# ELEMENTS AND COLOURS

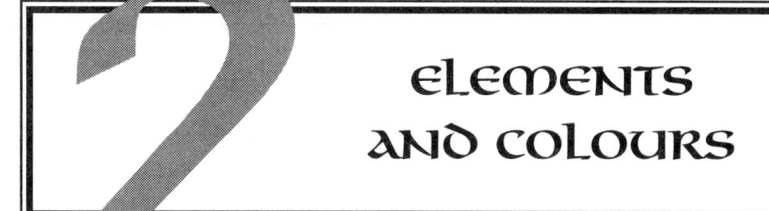

*One of the many misconceptions about Chinese face reading is that, because it was invented in China, it can have no possible application in the Western world. Chinese people, it is assumed, all have black hair, yellow skin and brown eyes, and therefore face reading must be a relatively short skill to learn. On the contrary, while spotting the difference between blue and brown eyes is perilously easy, Chinese face reading recognizes a myriad of differentiations and gradations. One of these is in the colour of the face.*

'Colour' in face reading is not concerned with ethnic origin – in fact, this is totally irrelevant. What interests a face reader is, all matters of ethnic origin considered, what other hue can be discerned on the face. Skin itself has no colour; it is the pigment in it that produces a black, white, brown, yellow or red face. What interests the face reader is the underlying influence. If the blood flows close to the surface of the skin, or the subject blushes easily, then the face will have a reddish tint. If the veins are prominent and close to the surface, it may have a bluish tint.

Note: discerning skin type can be quite difficult, and though it is presented first in this book (because it is traditionally the first part of face reading), you may find it easier to go onto the major features in subsequent chapters, and only come back to this when you have mastered those.

# FACE READING – A BEGINNER'S GUIDE

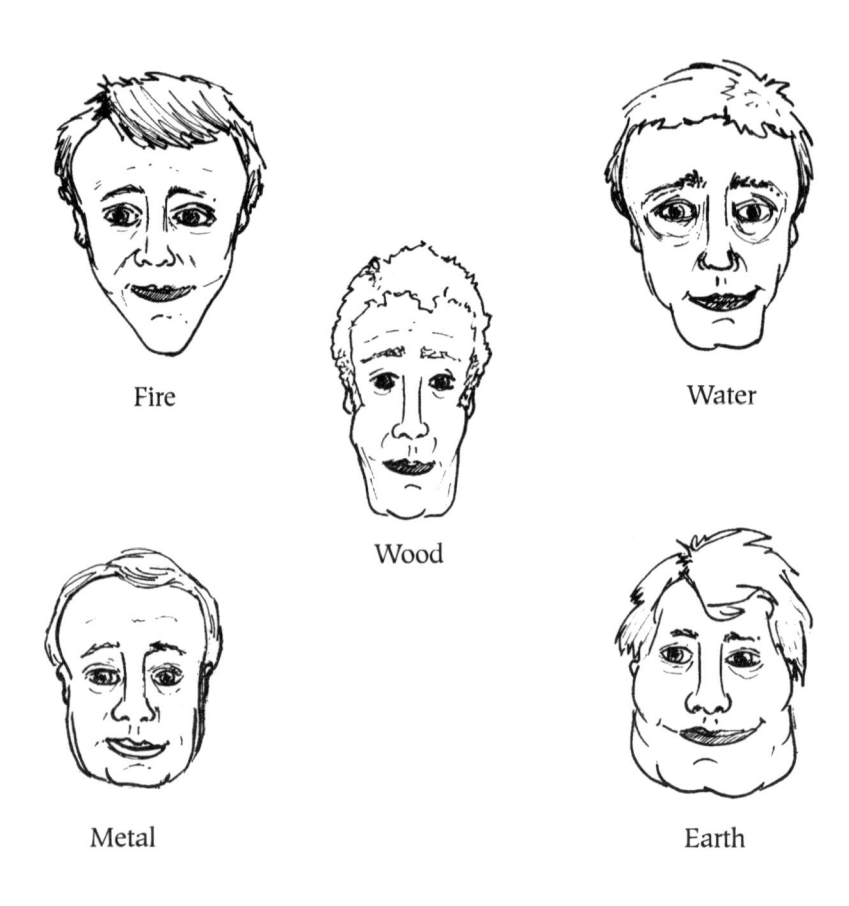

Fire

Water

Wood

Metal

Earth

Face shapes of the five elements.

# The Fire Element

If you find a redder tint in the face than usual, you have found a subject who is strong in the Fire element. This may be difficult to see immediately, but the Fire element also influences the actual shape of the face. A Fire face often looks like an inverted triangle, coming to a sharp point at the chin from a broad forehead.

The Fire person is passionate and active. Their tendency to grab any fuel they can find often results in hasty decisions. They often befriend the wrong people. In relationships, they can easily scare off potential partners with their all-or-nothing attitude – for example, whoever they end up blaming for marital difficulties, they may have to admit that it was their own fault for rushing into things before the fuel was there for a long-term blaze.

Though they may be a smoldering slow-burner, they contain the power to destroy forests, but are also often slow to act. Lighting a fire can take many tries, and getting a Fire person to do something they do not want to do can be as difficult as trying to spark wet tinder with flint and steel.

Dry skin and sore throats are the two ailments most likely to afflict a Fire person. They are likely to blaze out of control – a tendency that results in hot tempers and possibly overindulgence.

# The Water Element

The Water face is distinguished by a wide forehead and a large area of the face given over to the eyes (the face's most 'watery' feature). The addition of a jaw that tapers to a squarish chin has led many face readers to jokingly call this face-shape 'The Bucket'.

A blue tint to the skin can be caused by veins close to the surface of translucent, pale white skin. Conversely, it can also be discerned on black skin, so dark that it seems to have a bluey glow. Either form of bluish tint is an indicator that the subject is ruled by the Water element. As changeable and malleable as the sea, the Water person is sensitive – Chinese thought often ascribes a deep spirituality to the Water person. Conditions that cause runny noses or excess phlegm, such as catarrh or hay fever, are symptoms of the Water person, as is a tendency to bruise easily. This can be both literal and figurative – your feelings can be bruised just as easily as your body.

It is not a good idea to rely on a Water person in a crisis. Silent waters may run deep, but their attitude can be as changeable as the sea. The Water person contains multitudes – while they may seem quite normal and sociable, deep down they contain great lonely expanses. A Water person can seem solitary, even in the middle of a crowd.

Ironically, the Water person's luck in love is very similar to that of the Fire person. Both types rush right in without thinking, and often live to regret it. Although in the early stages a Water person may seem to get on well with their partner, they don't take kindly to being ordered around. They will eventually go their own way and find their natural course, and if this does not match the feelings or wishes of their partner, then it is quite likely that the Water person will simply flood and swell right past them.

# The Wood Element

The Wood element can be spotted in the colour green, although this is an extremely rare occurrence. It is far more likely to be discerned by the shape of the face – oblong, like a tall rectangle for men, or perhaps a more pronounced, tall oval for women. Wood signifies an attitude towards life like that of a tree putting out roots – slow but sure. While the Wood person may appear on the surface to be ineffectual, their gradual, long-term plans can buckle the strongest foundations or bear the sweetest fruits.

A Wood person may not be the first off the starting blocks, but they are the most likely to be the long-distance runners who win through sheer perseverance. Chinese folkore holds that the Wood person is determined, sometimes at the expense of others around them. Wood women demand all the attention; Wood men demand all the resources; both of them can be wilful and demanding in bed.

For Wood people, the worst dangers can come from their very steadfastness. A tall tree in the forest attracts both nesting birds and keen woodsmen with axes, and a successful Wood person must be wary of hangers-on and people out to exploit them. Because the roots are so essential for a tree, the feet are said to be the most likely places for a Wood person to be afflicted with ailments. They should be wary of athlete's foot, chilblains and ingrowing toenails.

Some face reading manuals use the terms 'Wood' and 'Jade' interchangeably – this is because the term 'Jade Face' is sometimes used as a euphemism for women with a Wood face. The 'Jade' emphasis may help you to remember the emphasis on green as a dominant colour.

# The Metal Element

The Metal face is shaped like an old-fashioned Chinese ingot – a square base and sides, with a domed or high forehead. Those ruled by the Metal element tend to be a lot paler in hue than other members of their race. A whitish tinge in the skin is a good indicator of the dominance of the Metal element.

Because it takes extreme heat to change Metal's shape, those who are ruled by this element are extremely good at hiding their feelings. They often strive for noble goals, but can also find their youthful idealism turning into greed as they age. Metal is the material that makes money (in Chinese, 'Gold' and 'Metal' are often interchangeable), a point that makes the Metal personality a razor-sharp investor. They often make excellent bankers, although they can all too often become obsessed by money to the extent that they can think of nothing else. The Metal person must be reminded often that all that glitters is not gold – they can easily become self-absorbed or miserly.

Metal people often have a heightened sense of justice (though they may plead that other forces prevent them from acting justly themselves). They are swift to criticize both themselves and others, though it is the others who are most likely to be wounded by the Metal person's sharp edges and uncompromising core.

The risks to the health of a Metal person are internal, in the minerals and vitamins that form part of our daily diet. A Metal person is most likely to benefit from a daily vitamin supplement, because in their rush to cut through the trials of the day, they often forget to eat properly, and risk their health in this way.

# The Earth Element

If someone is ruled by the Earth element, their face will be broader at the base than it is at the brow, but it will not taper to a recognizable point – the overall shape will be trapezoid. The dominant colours for someone heavily influenced by the Earth element are brown and yellow.

Earth faces are real towers of strength – like the land on which we stand, they possess the potential for infinite reliability and resources. Don't forget, of course, that in China the Earth is not always benign. If pushed to the limit, someone ruled by the Earth element can snap in a terrible fit of uncontrollable rage. Earthquakes may take hundreds of years to happen, but when they do finally occur, there is no stopping them. The Earth personality demands respect and integrity in all things, a desire for honourable treatment that is sometimes taken too far, becoming a certain bossiness and a belief that they really *are* the centre of the universe.

The Earth person often demonstrates an extreme confidence. This can make them reliable allies in a time of crisis, but they can also be set in their ways, convinced that their first hunch must be right, simply because they came up with it. In matters of health, they should be wary of what the Chinese sometimes call the 'rocks' of the body, which is to say the bones that provide the support for the skin and organs. Ailments of the bones and marrow are most likely to afflict someone of an Earth disposition, but forewarned is forearmed.

# The Interaction of the Elements

A ruling element is particularly useful in determining how two individuals will get on. The elements interact with each other in

# ELEMENTS AND COLOURS

different ways, and the future of a friendship, business venture or even relationship may depend quite heavily on the elemental leanings of the parties involved. The basics (along with the original rationales for such relationships) are listed below:

EARTH balances FIRE
because it is hardened and baked by the flames
METAL balances EARTH
because picks and shovels can overcome it
WATER balances METAL
because metal cannot resist rust
WOOD balances WATER
because it can absorb it and put it to use
FIRE balances WOOD
because wood feeds the flames

Balance is ideal in all things, and the above combinations of people are thought to be ideal. However, face reading is never that simple, because there are two other sets of elemental relationships. If the elements are not in a perfect, balanced position, then one of them will have the upper hand. At a basic level, this will mean that the individual with the dominant element is likely to be the dominant partner. As the book progresses, however, we will see that this is not necessarily the case. Someone with a dominant element as revealed by the face, might have other features that reveal a submissive character overall, and the various influences may cancel each other out:

FIRE weakens METAL
because only heat will melt it
METAL weakens WOOD
because saws and axes can cut it down
WOOD weakens EARTH
because tree roots push earth aside and sap its strength
EARTH weakens WATER
because it can soak it up without a trace
WATER weakens FIRE
because it can dowse the flames

## CASE STUDY

Everything about your impulsive, fiercely intelligent female friend says Fire. She is at a party, and three men also there are Water, Metal and Wood. Is there anything we can predict about the way they will interact?

Ms Fire and Mr Water just seem to be a damp squib. She exasperates him and he will eventually bore her to tears. If they are not careful, they may end up married and miserable!

Ms Fire is far more likely to be drawn to Mr Metal, because she will see him as a challenge. He may find her charming, but at some point, he's going to back off because he feels he is 'melting' – that might mean he's falling in love and it's time for him to change his lifestyle and go shopping for rings, or it might mean that she is cramping his style and he needs to finish things before she gets her hooks into him.

Mr Wood, meanwhile, is unlikely to think much of Ms Fire initially. He will find her loud, brash, a little too forward perhaps, and generally annoying. She won't even notice he's there. He will make a point of telling everyone how annoying she is, and when it is time for everyone to go home, you will discover the two of them in a clinch in the cloakroom. They are simply made for each other because she is a firecracker and he is a slow-burner, and between them they have much to teach each other.

# 3 Major Single Features

*There are three levels to face reading: the overall colour of the complexion; the major features that remain relatively constant; the minor features that can alter with great rapidity. The complexion sets the general direction, the major features fill in the specifics, and the minor areas define areas of detail such as actual types of behaviour and influences on particular areas of the subject's fate.*

## The Nose

In Chinese thought, the nose has always been the foremost part of the face. This is why in China to this day, a leader or innovator is referred to as a 'nose-ancestor', because they lead the pack just that little bit ahead of everyone else. Since the nose is at the centre of the face, it is also sometimes referred to as the 'centre of life'.

Face readings for the nose usually revolve around financial matters – the fleshy part at the tip is looked upon as a money bag, and the nostrils as the holes in it that govern spending habits. A bulbous nose denotes great wealth, a thin pointed one means meagre savings, but neither of these readings is the whole story. If your nostrils are large, you might be immensely wealthy but will never have any money as you will spirit away all your money. Conversely, if you have little money but the tiny nostrils of a miser, you may well still manage to keep all your accounts in the black.

## Roman

The Roman nose, with its slight crook and beak-like tip, is regarded as a symbol of hawk-like nobility. The owner of the Roman nose is shrewd and sharp, a fighter and a calculator. Always looking for a cause to rally round in the poltical or business world, in relationship matters they are intrigued by a challenge. Insatiable in their desires for sexual experimentation, they are often sexual athletes – if they are not careful, such conspicuous achievements may come at the expense of true feeling, both for them and for others.

## Hooked

The hooked nose is a symbol of unbeatable business acumen. Its owner has a real hunger for promotion and success. Whether they find it by legal or illegal means (the nose does not say – other parts of the face determine such matters...), they will be adept at manipulating the system to their advantage. They make excellent lawyers and bankers, and, because their understanding of systems is so practical, superb teachers. They make excellent spouses, because they are choosy with their partners and often ensure that when they sign on the dotted line on a marriage contract, both they and their partner understand exactly what sort of deal they are entering into. For the same reason, they can be unlucky in love – if other parts of the face make them less choosy about their other halves, they can often be disappointed when others refuse to play by the rules. In relationships in younger life, where, frankly, there *are* no rules, hooked noses are often disappointed, but they should be consoled by the knowledge that life for them is an upward curve towards the better.

## Snub

The diametrical opposite of the hooked nose, the snub nose is a symbol of guile and self-deception. In the financial matters with which the nose is chiefly concerned, it can be very bad news indeed – a snub nose denotes a person with little control over their own

Roman nose

Bumpy nose

Hooked nose

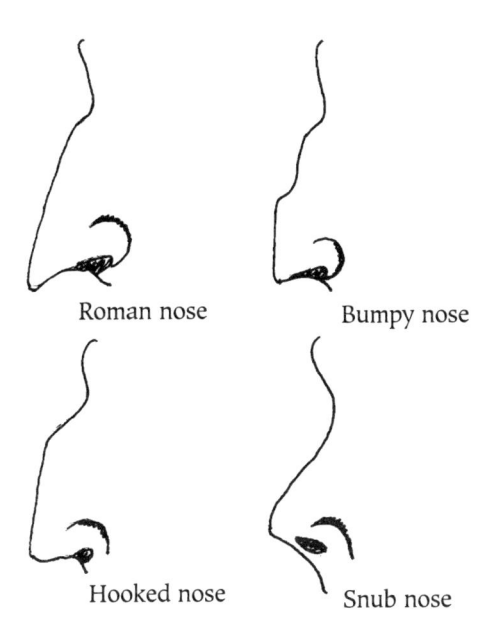

Snub nose

finances, liable to waste money on extravagances and forget to save in times of plenty. The owner of a snub nose is a dreamer and a butterfly, just as desirous of promotion and advancement as anyone else, but far less likely to achieve it. They genuinely enjoy life, often at the expense of their career, and their naïvety will win them many friends (and, unfortunately, many unscrupulous exploiters). In affairs of the heart, they give themselves unreservedly, regardless of whether their paramour is deserving of such affection.

## Bumpy

Regardless of the nose's overall shape, some types are distinguished by an uneven surface. The owner of such a nose is stubborn and opinionated, and very unlikely to change their mind on any subject about which they feel passionately. The Chinese mistrust of a bumpy nose stems from its association with brawling and argument – if the nose looks like it has been broken through fights or accidents, then this suggests a pugnacious individual. Some Chinese manuals regard this nose as the mark of a true fighter and a noble warrior, whereas other analyses point out that a truly good soldier wouldn't have any scars at all!

## The Bridge

Check also for the bridge of a person's nose. Regardless of the type of nose, where does it actually begin? A nose that begins high on the forehead is another sign of supreme success in money matters, regardless of where the owner started out. The owner of a high nose will achieve great success out of nothing if born into poverty, and enrich their family tenfold if born into wealth.

Conversely, even if someone with a low bridge is born into privilege, they will turn out to be the wastrel who fritters away the family fortune. The low bridge, often in conjunction with a snub nose (see above), is a sign of a supreme lack of ability at managing money. No matter how many lucky breaks come their way, this person will never be able to capitalize on them. They make for terrible bankers and financiers – just hope that the other aspects of their face suggest success in other areas!

## Width

A sharp, thin, shrewish nose is the sign of someone who is critical and cutting. They are difficult to please and are easily spooked or stressed. It can also be a sign of refinement, but the very delicacy associated with a thin nose is part of the high-minded attitude that can lead to the subject's dissatisfaction with others.

A broad, flat nose, however, is the sign of someone who is not afraid to take life easy. Though their nose still precedes them through life like everyone else's, it can give them substantial cushioning against life's trials. They are easily pleased and rarely complain.

## MAJOR SINGLE FEATURES

> ### CASE STUDY
>
> Your friend is buying a house. He has a large, wide, bumpy nose with a bulbous tip, small nostrils and a high bridge. His face is pale and clearly Metal-influenced. At a rough guess, how do you think he will fare?
>
> His nose doesn't demonstrate any particular sense of business acumen, but luck does seem to be a major factor in his monetary fate. The relation of nostrils to tip implies that he actually has a lot more money than he thinks – the surprise extra payments involved in house-buying are not going to bankrupt him. The high bridge implies that he ought to get a good deal (more by luck than judgement), but what about the bumpy surface? He is a stubborn individual – perhaps everything is going to work out, but is he buying the *right* house? Will he want to stay there? Has he bought the right kind of mortgage? These are likely to be things he has not considered, since he has been so busy arranging everything else. As his face reader, these are the questions you should be bringing to his attention.

# The mouth

The mouth is one of the most elastic parts of the face. It is relatively easy to alter its shape and consistency, unlike most other features. Lips can change colour over time, teeth can distort the outer appearance, and the tensing or relaxation of the facial muscles can literally change the mouth's size and shape. This unique changeability has made the mouth a very sensual part of any face reading. It has always been associated in China with emotion – the mouth is not just used for kissing and tasting food; it is the last portal that feelings cross before they are irrevocably spoken as words. The mouth can hold the water of the body like a reservoir, it can leak in the presence of excess of emotion, or become parched when the subject thirsts – for something to drink, or perhaps some other craving.

Even without speaking, the mouth and lips can tell us much about the owner's feelings. Thin, drawn lips are a sign of stress or worry, likewise a downturned mouth. The superficial forms of expression (a smile or frown) are not our concern; we are more interested in the peripheral qualities of supposedly obvious things – a smile can be sad, and tears can be of joy.

## Size

A large mouth is a sign of a ravenous, fearless hunger, not just for food, but for all kinds of oral pleasures. The owner of a big mouth is a big talker, a great eater and a hungry lover. But this trait only concerns itself with quantity – there's no guarantee that this overwhelming need will recognize the difference between good and bad conversation, food or partners. Check also how the size of the mouth relates to the size of the ears. A good talker is not necessarily a good listener. The large-mouthed person will be an extrovert and forthright person – sometimes a little too forthright, since they may have no qualms about complaining about anything and everything. In affairs of the heart they are often self-centred, but will repay anyone who can ring their bell with a passionate loyalty.

Conversely, a small mouth is a sign of an introverted, careful personality. Though they may have more of interest to say than their loud-mouthed companions, they may never say it. This could be due to shyness, or perhaps even a snobbish sense of *hauteur* – just because the small-mouthed person is a wallflower, it does not follow that they will be grateful for *any* attention. Tight-lipped in more ways than one, the owner of a small mouth is good at keeping secrets, sometimes to the extent of keeping grievances quiet when they really should be voiced to clear the air. In relationships they can be infuriatingly uncommunicative, and their partner will need to understand that they value their solitude and their privacy.

When applied to the subject's sexual relationships, the size of the mouth is thought to relate directly to the time it takes the subject to reach orgasm – the larger the mouth, the more time the subject needs. In general, when it comes to keeping one's partner entertained, a small mouth is a good thing in a woman and a bad thing in a man.

## Lips

If both the lips are of equal size, then we simply talk about them as part of the mouth's size (see above). However, if one of the lips is larger than the other, we can read a little more into the person's sensual nature. If the upper lip is thicker than the lower lip, or protrudes beyond it, it gives the impression (or indeed, it may actually be the case) that the owner is sucking, ever so slightly, on their lower lip. Universally, this is a sign of nerves, and can be a sign of insincerity. The person with this kind of mouth is hiding something, and it is the kind of thing that they do not want you to discover. The thicker upper lip is the mark of the serial seducer, a tireless seeker after sensual pleasure. However, unlike the person whose lips are simply large and erotic, this person must always put effort into their seductions. Are they seeking the wrong person? Or is it that their very insincerity has made it impossible to charm someone else without literally lying? Only a consultation of the rest of the face can answer these questions.

If the lower lip is thicker than the upper lip, or protrudes beyond it, the Chinese face reader sees a different kind of facial tick. It gives the impression that the owner is sucking thoughtfully on their upper lip – a sign of sensibility, though perhaps also a sign of cool calculation.

People whose lower lip is thicker than the upper are often likely to feel hard-done-by. Ever calculating how to improve their lot in life, they are rarely satisfied with a particular rank, wage or even partner. Natural leaders but terrible followers, they are often unlucky in love, not because they do not meet the right sort of person, but because they are always tempted to try for someone better, whether their current relationship is working or not.

## Pouting

All over the world, a pout is a symbol of sensuality and sulking, and the two often go together. If both lips appear frozen in a pout, a Chinese face reader will reach the same conclusion as anyone else: that the subject is vain and perhaps arrogant.

It's not quite as simple as that, however (face reading never is!), because the source of the vanity is open to debate. The person might be a natural beauty, or high-born gentry, used to getting their own way, and only likely to sulk when they do not. Or, they may be someone with ideas above their station – only reading the rest of the face can determine these things.

The sensuality of a pouter is difficult to unlock. In the early stages of a relationship, they will welcome attention because it confirms their own self-interest, but sex itself may seem like too much effort. They may be willing to receive, but the act of giving is almost an anathema to them. The pouter in a relationship is most likely to regard every loving act as a form of transaction, everything that others would give freely as a minor annoyance to be endured in return for some other service.

## Lip Alignment

If the corners of the mouth turn up, the face seems frozen in a permanent smile. As you might expect, this is regarded as a symbol of well-being and good fortune. Such people are often a self-fulfilling prophecy – they are optimistic and sociable and hence rarely want for friends or lovers. Stress management is ingrained into this type of person – no matter how bad their life becomes, they are always ready to face each new day with a smile and get on with setting things straight. In matters where you want honest advice, they may be your worst enemy, because they often fail to see anything but the good side. If there is a downside at all, it is that their positive outlook, and seemingly effortless success, may often attract the attention of lame ducks. Sometimes, despite all their extrovert charm, they will want to be left alone to recharge.

Conversely, downturned corners imply a permanent state of misery. These people are often shy and solitary – they have the uncanny ability to see the bad side of any situation, and this attitude often scares potential friends away. Many people are unwilling to hear the brutal truth – they try to ignore the dark clouds gathering on the horizon – but the owner of a downturned mouth is fearlessly honest.

## MAJOR SINGLE FEATURES

If you find yourself taking advice from someone with this sort of mouth, remember that they are often the only person foolhardy enough to speak the truth, no matter how unpalatable you may find it. Be aware that they also see a bright, sunny day and think only of sunburn and wasps.

A subject with a crooked mouth is very vocal, both in and out of bed. They love to talk and flirt, and the strange shape of their mouth is liable to attract onlookers, almost hypnotically. The attention they get, and their readiness to discuss private matters so frankly, often makes them popular – both sexes with this feature often have trouble remaining monogamous, purely due to the many tempting situations in which they find themselves.

# Teeth

The teeth are the inner strength that lies behind the emotional ebb and flow of the lips. For this reason, they are often associated in face reading with someone's internal workings.

The teeth are also an extremely good indicator of general health. Even in a modern society, with dentistry and toothpaste, people's ability to look after their teeth varies considerably. Bright, white, strong teeth are the sign of someone who has taken active care of themselves from an early age – it is fair to assume they take a similar interest in the health of the rest of their body. Yellowing, cracked, uneven teeth are the sign of someone who has taken less care, for whatever reason. They may be a smoker, they may be poor, they may regard advanced dentistry as a frivolous expense, but whatever their reason, it is likely to apply to the rest of their body too. A beautiful set of teeth can be bought, that much is true, but the kind of person who is prepared to pay for good teeth is also the kind of person who will be taking similar interest in other areas of healthcare.

Unique in the face for being underneath the skin and yet still visible, the teeth are a means of understanding a person's innermost attitudes. Someone born with bad teeth learns early on not to smile too broadly or laugh too loudly – even as a child, they begin to learn the value of discretion and silence. This superficial concern can take root deep down and become a self-fulfilling prophecy. Just as someone who wears glasses is less likely to risk breaking them on the sports field, and hence more likely to grow into a bookish stereotype, someone with bad teeth is likely to be withdrawn and introverted.

Great teeth make for a great smile, and a smile that the owner is not afraid to flash around. They bring confidence and self-awareness, and a certain boldness in life, business and love. Other features of the teeth are more liable to be occluded. If someone has had dental work, the chances of seeing what the work hides are remote, to say the least. But if you believe your subject to be relatively free from dental interference, the teeth may have much to teach you.

Universally, small teeth resemble the milk teeth of a child – a trait that is often reflected in the subject's other behaviours. They may charm others unwittingly with their acts, but ultimately they are only out for their own interests – their preferred method of getting their own way is to beg others' indulgence or feign incompetence.

Universally, large teeth are a sign of success (especially in business) but not without effort. This is because the teeth are ready to smile, but that does not necessarily guarantee that the lips are already in position to make that happen. Such people will also be out for their own ends, but are not adverse to helping others on the way up, since they are well aware that they may meet them on the way down.

## Animal Features

Long teeth are an easy feature to remember, since the Chinese too have the concept of being 'long in the tooth'. People with this feature have fiercely accurate memories and quickly gain vast reservoirs of knowledge, but this very intelligence often makes them slow and indecisive. They will think through every possible angle of a problem before doing anything – a trait that brings mixed blessings.

If the teeth protrude outwards, the face reading will refer to these as 'goat teeth'. By reaching just that little bit closer to the ground, a goat's teeth permit the animal to graze on much sparser ground than other creatures, meaning they can live in harsher conditions and even re-graze land that cattle seem to have already grazed clean. In human face reading, the ownership of goat's teeth is seen as a sign of a gregarious character, but also a person given to outstanding stubbornness.

If the teeth slope inwards, they will appear like those of a shark, designed to make it impossible for prey to struggle free without further injury. Owners of shark's teeth are liable to bite and then hold on, in all aspects of their life. They have trouble letting go even when all sense dictates that it is the sensible option – this can make them possessive or blinkered lovers. Like the shark that they resemble, they are often likely to be solitary creatures, spurning the herd-like instincts of their opposite numbers with goat's teeth. The owner of shark's teeth may often prove to be too intense for others to handle. They may find themselves respected, but perhaps also shunned.

Two large front teeth in an otherwise normal mouth are the sign of someone who always needs reassurance and support from others. The face reading is based on animal lore – their teeth resemble a chipmunk's who, by gnawing on wood, exposes the most heartfelt emotions (the mouth and teeth) to outside scrutiny. These people wear their hearts on their sleeves, and expect others to notice that they are always genuine. Such honesty often leads to stubbornness and impatience – they do not understand why everyone cannot immediately see the world their way.

Two large incisors are the symbol of someone with the cunning of a wolf and the tenacity of a vampire. Such fangs represent a skilful manipulator of others, but also someone who can become incredibly defensive of their motives – if wronged, they can hold a grudge for a very long time indeed.

## Spacing

If the teeth are widely spaced in the mouth, with a noticeable gap in between them, a face reader will say there are also gaps in their decisions. No smile is 100 per cent smile; no growl is 100 per cent growl – the subject will often have trouble making up their mind.

Even after they have reached a decision, they will often retain a niggling doubt that they have made the wrong decision. They will seek the advice of others, not only because it saves them having to decide for themselves, but because if the choice later turns out to be wrong, they will have someone else to blame for a mistake that, at the heart of the matter, is all their own.

## CASE STUDY

A male friend is not sure if a female acquaintance likes him, and you bring face reading to bear on the problem. They went on a date, and he confesses that she did most of the talking, while he stared entranced at her crooked mouth. She has two prominent front teeth (not overly so, but he noticed because the rest of her teeth were rather small) and he thinks that her teeth protrude outwards ever-so-slightly. When she kissed him goodbye, it was quite wet and slobbery, even though it was just a peck on the cheek. Ideally, you would like more information, but he was so distracted by her mouth, the only other things he can remember is that her face seemed redder than normal (suggesting she is ruled by the Fire element) and that she had a small, snub nose. What do you think?

She is impulsive and emotional (we get that from the Fire nature and the wet mouth), but does she really know what she wants at all? She has the snub nose and small teeth of a child who wants someone to take the lead, or may even be unconsciously leading him on. The crooked mouth and the chipmunk teeth are both good indicators that she would not be afraid to take the leading role in a relationship – the fact that she did not initiate anything suggests she is not that interested in him. She has the gregarious teeth of a goat, so maybe she is just looking for companionship. This women is not afraid to make the first move – the chances are quite high that if she did not bring up the subject of relationships, she wanted to talk to him about something else.

# 4 DOUBLE FEATURES

*The majority of the features of the human face exist in pairs, but pure symmetry is incredibly rare. You can see this for yourself by placing a mirror halfway across a photograph of a face. When the left of the face is reflected back on the left, or the right against the right, you will see a very different face, even on a photo of yourself. Face reading makes use of the left and right sides of the face in much the same way that palmistry divides the left and right hands into inherited and acquired traits.*

## The ears

The ears reveal a subject's potential and future career. For this reason, they are most important when reading a young face – though our potential is continually changing until the day we die, few of us deviate from a particular path once we become adults.

As a part of the body that contains blood but no bones, and that can be viewed from an angle that has nothing (no skull, no shadows) behind it, the ear is also an excellent indicator of feelings. The colour of the ear can change quite radically – it is often a good thing to check this when first meeting with someone new, because the changes will be more easily recognized if the person suddenly becomes angry or embarrassed. On these occasions, the increased blood flow around the body will be most noticeable in the ears, which will turn redder than usual.

## Shape

A normal ear-shape is rectangular. The ear will be taller than its own width with dimensions that remain constant all the way up. The usefulness of the ear in determining something beyond an 'average' fate comes when we can see how far it deviates from this norm.

### Top-heavy

If the top of the ear is wider than the base, this makes for excellent hearing. There's no philosophical rationale for this, but a scientific one – we can see its practical application in the modern-day construction of radar dishes. This person's slight advantage over others when it comes to hearing will also impact on other areas of their personality – their alertness and intuition is also above average. Though it may only make the tiniest daily difference, over the course of their life the advantages will slowly increase. Maybe one time in a thousand, the word or number that others mishear will be heard by them at a moment when it counts, or the sound of incoming danger (be it on the street or in the edge in someone's voice) will spur them to get out of trouble just a split-second before their aurally-inferior colleagues. Ultimately, this fractionally advantageous access to better information or education will make them faster at coming up with new ideas. They are also more likely to pick up tiny tell-tale signals in someone's voice that allows them a better chance at hearing the stress and nerves that come when someone is lying to them.

### Base-heavy

If the base of the ear is wider than the top, the face reading is one of heightened wisdom. The power of the ear is directed inwards, at the subject's own thoughts and feelings, and they are liable to spend much time in contemplation of their own inner mind. The owner of base-heavy ears, while taking much longer to come to decisions than their quick-witted, lightning-reflexed, top-heavy counterpart, can still think through the important issues with considerably more detail. Whereas the top-heavy subject is quick to reach important conclusions about others, the base-heavy subject is able to assemble an equally large reservoir of self-knowledge. Although they may occasionally spend too much time prevaricating, their knowledge of themselves is peerless, and whatever decisions they reach are liable to benefit themselves in the long term.

### Round

If the general shape of the ear is neither rectangular nor irregular, but round, it is a mark of creativity. Like the yin-yang symbol it superficially resembles, the round ear is a sign of someone who is at peace with the spiritual nature of the universe, and able to tap into that harmony with creative expression. The owner of round ears is much more likely to be artistically minded, and can achieve great success in a creative profession such as art, literature or music. There is a downside – this spiritual nature goes hand-in-hand with a marked inability to comprehend material things. The owner of round ears is likely to go into business and investment with rose-tinted glasses – their creative nature often means that they see the best in everyone, even potential business rivals.

## Alignment

Animal iconography comes to the fore in ear alignment. If the ears stick out conspicuously like the wings of a butterfly, the subject's own personality is likely to be as ephemeral and carefree as one of these gentle insects. Effortlessly graceful, the subject may also prove to be flighty and easily-swayed, particularly in career matters (the area that the ears rule above all others). In all things, but especially career matters, the owner of butterfly ears is likely to spend too much time enjoying the warm summer, and may give too little thought to the coming winter until it is too late.

Conversely, ears that are pinned back tightly against the head, like those of a nervous horse, are a sign of a jittery personality. Ever nervous and fretful, this person exercises extreme caution, often to such a great extent that they never get anything done at all. Such people may often require leading by the reins.

# Relative size and position

According to face reading lore, if you look at your subject's face straight-on, a normal ear will be level with the eyebrows at the top, and level with the base of the nose at the bottom. If the size and position of the ears exceeds both these limits (in other words, if they are exceptionally large) this is a sign of a person with a bright, outgoing personality. If the size and position of the ears falls below these limits in both cases (in other words, if the ears are exceptionally small) they are likely to be more shy and reserved.

If the ears are placed higher on the head (beginning above the base of the nose and rising to a point above the brows) it is a sign of complacent living. Someone with this kind of ear is happy with their lot in life, unwilling to stand out in a crowd or make a fuss about anything. Sometimes, their happiness may be a trifle misleading – they may pretend to be satisfied because the alternative is to admit that something has to be done, and these people are not the kind to want to roll up their sleeves and get involved.

If the ears sit lower on the head (beginning below the base of the nose and rising to a point below the brows), it is a sign of an outgoing and gregarious individual. Never happy unless they are running with the herd, these people are sociable and go-getting. Unlike their high-eared opposites, they are always striving for betterment in all walks of life, and are no stranger to hard work. This does not necessarily mean that they are unhappy – just that they will freely admit when things are not 100 per cent perfect, and if a job is really worth doing, it's worth doing yourself.

Small ears (beginning above the base of the nose and finishing below the brows) are the sign of a tough individual who, while they may or may not get on with others, will ultimately have to fend for themselves in all matters. The owner of small ears needs to learn to look after number one, because no-one else is going to do it for them.

Large ears (beginning below the base of the nose and finishing above the brow line) are the sign of excellent prospects. The owner of such ears is a born leader, shrewd at business and able to handle the responsibilities and pressures that their generally good fortune will bring them. They are also extremely good at dealing with others – sociable and polite, they are the kind of friends you can take anywhere, into any situation, and know they will land on their feet.

## Wheels of Fortune

Human ears are divided by face reading into three component parts – the lobe, the inner wheel and the outer wheel.

### Outer Wheel

The outer wheel, that ridge around the long edge of the ear, can inform a face reader about someone's personality. If it is thick and fleshy, it is the sign of an earthy person who rates the body over the mind. Such a person is more likely to be interested in physical sports (though not necessarily as a participant – they may prefer to watch others exert themselves), or physical pleasures such as chocolate, exercise or sex. Their worst enemy is overindulgence.

If the outer wheel is thin and sharp, like the edge of a knife, it is a sign that the owner is quick-witted. They prefer intellectual stimulation to the physical, and value mind over matter. They are more likely to keep their heads while all around are losing theirs. It is the mind that interests these people – in sporting matters they prefer strategy over brute force, and the pleasures they enjoy tend to be more cerebral. Their worst enemy is perhaps their tendency to take this too far, seeking what they think they want, such as cultured entertainment, at the expense of what they really want.

There is a rare, third type of outer wheel, which occurs when the wheel ends in an elfin point rather than a smooth arc. Owners of such pointed ears emphasize the spiritual above the physical or the intellectual, demonstrating great intuitive abilities and an understanding of hidden depths. Such ears can be a sign of paranormal abilities or a sixth sense, but also of a subject with their head perpetually in the clouds. They may be able to gauge others' feelings on sight, but they are just as likely to be so busy contemplating the infinite that they do not notice when others around them need their help. Their worst enemy is losing touch with the real world.

### The Inner Wheel

The inner wheel, that ridge of cartilage around the ear hole, is an indicator of social behaviour. If it is so prominent as to extend further outwards than the rest of the ear, then the owner is an extrovert. If it is lower and flatter, then the owner is an introvert.

## Earlobe

The lobe of the ear is an indicator of wisdom, and, by association, the length of one's life. The Buddha's earlobes are traditionally thought to be very long and fleshy, and over time this has come to mean that the longer and fatter the lobes, the longer the lifespan the subject can expect, and the greater the wisdom they can expect to attain.

An integral part of wisdom is respect for others and acknowledgement that oneself is not the centre of the universe. This is why the earlobe of the wise person will be almost separate from the body. Some people may have large lobes that remain attached to the side of the head by a piece of skin. These are a sign of someone with knowledge and cunning, but who is only prepared to use it for their own ends.

## Hairy

Hairy ears are a sign of someone whose natural abilities are fogged by an inability to listen to well-meaning criticism. Although they are often of an academic bent, they rarely place any value on the opinions of others, and although they may find themselves knowing a little about anything, putting that knowledge into practice is often beyond them.

## Case study

An urgent phone call drags you out of the office for the rest of the afternoon, at exactly the wrong time. An important client is coming to visit, and you're going to have to delegate what you were doing over to one of your subordinates. Mr A has ears pinned back tightly to the side of his head, but with protuding inner wheels. This makes him nervous and flighty, but with an outgoing nature and an abililty to get on with people. Mr B has large ears that stick out, making him alert to problems, but he is also likely to forget exactly what the problems are. Ms C has small ears with long, dangly lobes, which make her shy, but also wise. Who should you delegate to?

The answer really depends on who is coming, the nature of your business and how they are likely to react. An important new client is probably best dealt with by Ms C, since however badly things go, she will be able to make the best of the situation and say the right thing. Someone who knows your business better, or is simply dropping in on a regular basis, would be best entertained by Mr A, who can make nervous excuses about the mess and your absence, but nevertheless keep them entertained and look after their needs. Mr B isn't really suitable for looking after visitors. He is better off actually on the operations business, dealing with any short-term problems that come in, keeping everything on an even keel. Each of these employees has their own strengths and weaknesses, but it is face reading that can help you determine what they are.

# The eyes

As another soft, mutable part of the face, like the mouth, the eyes are another indicator of deep feelings. They tell us about the subject's emotional disposition, their intelligence and, sometimes, their temper. Although there are readings for the colour of the iris, these are a relatively recent invention – traditional face reading prefers to concentrate on other features, such as the shape and the disposition of the whites of the eyes. Both kinds of reading are included below.

## Colour

Human eye colour can be divided up into the following broad categories:

- **Blue eyes** show someone who is outgoing and honest, in fact, someone who finds it difficult to lie. Blue is the colour of a promise-keeper.
- **Green eyes** are the colour of jade, and hence the sign of a spiritual power beyond normal understanding. Someone with green eyes will have excellent intuitive abilities, and a sense of fair play that may often backfire. Jade can be broken, but never twisted, and this attitude comes across in the green-eyed person's attitude towards life. The stories of the 'green-eyed monster' are not necessarily tales of jealousy run riot, but someone, unprepared to compromise, who has suddenly snapped and let their true feelings come out.
- **Brown eyes** are a symbol of normality. Strong and reliable, the owner of brown eyes is down-to-earth and matter-of-fact. They are unimpressed by others' posturing – they are doers not talkers, and brash boasts will not sway them.
- **Grey eyes** (a colour that includes all the grey-greens, blue-greens, hazels and other very light hues) are symbols of constant change. Like the sea that they resemble, these eyes denote a personality in a permanent state of flux. Sometimes calm, sometimes stormy, these people remain eternally unable to make up their minds about anything. They are always unpredictable. The eyes themselves may seem to change colour when the subject puts on different coloured clothes. Such a chameleon-like property can be expected to come across in other aspects of their life – they have an uncanny ability to blend into any situation.

## Depth of colour

Colour represents the depth of emotion a person is capable of experiencing, especially in bed. The darker the eyes, the greater the passion. Lighter eyes may still denote an individual who is friendly and gregarious, but they may well be too self-regarding to really let themselves go in bed.

## Whites of eyes

In China, where the homogeneity of eye colour makes it difficult to distinguish the tiny variations in the colour of the iris, face readers prefer to concentrate on the white of the eye. The normal eye is said to have an iris that neatly fills the top and bottom quadrants, showing a little amount of white on either side. But the presence of unbalanced amounts of white in the eye will allow for some detailed face readings, as detailed below.

If the eye has more white beneath it than above it, it gives the subject the aspect of a bull with head lowered to charge. The subject's reading is one of a fierce temper and an anger that sometimes gets the better of them. They will also be someone who, once their mind is set on something, is almost impossible to deter. Whether or not they are charging straight for a wall, they are apt to give their all in any task.

Conversely, someone with a large amount of white above the eye, but little or none below it, will have their eyes set in a position that gives the impression they are looking snootily down on the world. Quick to criticize others, but reluctant ever to turn that strong sensibility onto their own failings, such people are never satisfied. Although they may appear to be perfectly polite and friendly, the chances are high that this gentility is an indirect sleight on you – they are sociable towards you because it is 'the done thing', not necessarily because they genuinely like you.

An eye that is surrounded by very little white at all is the sign of a focused and directed individual – it looks as if the coloured part of their eye is 'zooming' in on the world around them. Even if they feign a ditzy and disorganized personality, they are in fact far more aware of their surroundings than they may be letting on. Such people have an ability to appraise others on sight that penetrates deep into your soul. Sometimes, they can tell your secrets just by looking into your eyes. However, in practical, day-to-day life, they may suffer from a narrowness of vision. While they are able to dissect something directly in front of them with an impressive pinpoint accuracy, they are liable to forget about peripheral issues – they can be the literal personification of the Chinese maxim: 'Beware, lest your eyes are bigger than your head.' At a buffet, they make take more food than they could reasonably be expected to eat. In other areas of life, they are similarly liable to bite off more than they can chew.

An eye that seems surrounded by acres of white, not just on either side, but with white showing both above and below the iris, gives the appearance of someone whose eyes are eternally open in surprise. Such people are liable to go through life hearing shocking news at every turn – they run heavy risks of health problems.

One of the contributing factors to their eternal surprise is not so much a miraculously strange lifestyle or fortune, but the simple fact that they rarely concentrate on the matter in hand. Their attention is liable to wander at crucial moments. They are easily bored, and are often mystified when a danger that has been obvious to everyone else jumps up and hits them in the face. In affairs of the heart, they are often doomed to pick partners who can run rings around them. They should watch out for infidelities on the part of their other half, and also take time to listen to their partner's feelings. If they do not, they risk using that look of continual surprise at home, when they walk in the front door to discover their spouse has moved out and taken all the furniture.

## Size

Big eyes are a sign of beauty, but also of childlike innocence. Such people are often at the centre of attention, and attract many members of the opposite sex. They can also demonstrate considerable immaturity in their relationships – they want everything, *now*! Whether they know it or not, they often need to be led by the hand through whatever difficulties they may experience. Often gullible or capricious, their innocence can be turned to evil ends by those who are not ashamed to exploit them. However, when they are cared for and nurtured, they will blossom into beautiful, intelligent, noble people.

Small eyes are a sign of an intensely private individual. They are fiercely loyal, not just to people, but to abstract ideals. This may lead to behaviour that others find strange or overly picky, and the person with small eyes is often wrongly mistrusted simply for standing by their guns. People with small eyes flourish in a bureaucratic work environment, where their dogged hard work is noticed over time, along with their tight-lipped refusal to brag about it. However, such long-term success is unlikely to be reflected in their work relationships, where those they share an office with will soon pigeonhole them as a nag and a stickler.

## Position

Upward-slanting eyes are regarded as the ultimate sign of beauty and good fortune. Called 'phoenix eyes' in women and 'dragon eyes' in men, they are a sign of supreme intelligence, long life and free emotions. As with all rare breeds, their temperament can be difficult – women are often fickle and demanding, while men are given to rages when things do not go their own way. They are the long-distance runners of the career world, meeting difficulties head-on and enjoying well-deserved success in their late thirties and beyond.

Downward-slanting eyes often make a person look uncomfortable, as if they are holding back tears. They are a sign of someone who often has to overcome misfortune – but nevertheless, they are a sign of someone who overcomes it, and does not succumb to it. Symbolic of someone who will prevail over a tough early start in their career, they are also gentle and passive. A listener rather than a talker, the owner of downward-slanting eyes never takes the lead, even when circumstances dictate they should be bolder and more assertive.

## Spacing

Animal imagery comes to the fore again with the spacing of the eyes. Some people have eyes set very far apart, and, like those animals with such eyes taken to extremes, Chinese face reading holds that they are very good at seeing everything all around them, apart from, in crucial moments, when the thing is right in front of their nose. While friendly and gregarious, these people can also be gullible and naïve.

Close-set eyes are another problem entirely. These people are able to focus on what is in front of them with pinpoint accuracy. They know what they want and they know how to get it, but sometimes their persistence in one area of their fortune will leave them blinkered in other areas. The person with close-set eyes often suffers from tunnel vision in their fate – although, unlike the person with wide-set eyes, they have a razor sharp sense when it comes to dealing with would-be deceivers, they can be tripped up by circumstances that are simply unforeseen. They are liable to rush into a situation without thinking of the ramifications, and often see only one side of a story, be it good or bad.

## Sockets

Another face reading can be taken from the relative position of the eyes and the sockets. If the eyes are deep-set, the dark, brooding look denotes a person with a deep sense of the romantic and the passionate. They are no stranger to intellectual depths either, and score high on any kind of intelligence test. In bed, they are considerate and thoughtful partners.

If the eyes sit very high on the sockets, giving a protruding or 'bug-eyed' appearance, the face reading is far less positive. The Chinese like to say that such a person's eyes enter the room before them – they are ever willing to plot and scheme to their own advantage. Often with little thought for anyone but themselves, their incredibly strong willpower often brings them great success in professional spheres, even if such success comes at the expense of many long-lasting friendships. Men with such eyes often risk becoming sex addicts, since they are rarely satisfied with whatever partner they may already have, no matter how wonderful they may be. Women also change partners regularly, but are apt to be taken in by any person who knows how to appeal to their innate vanity. No matter how strong the relationship they may find themselves in, they are liable to drop it all if someone arrives who seems richer, more successful or with greater potential.

## Other eye shapes

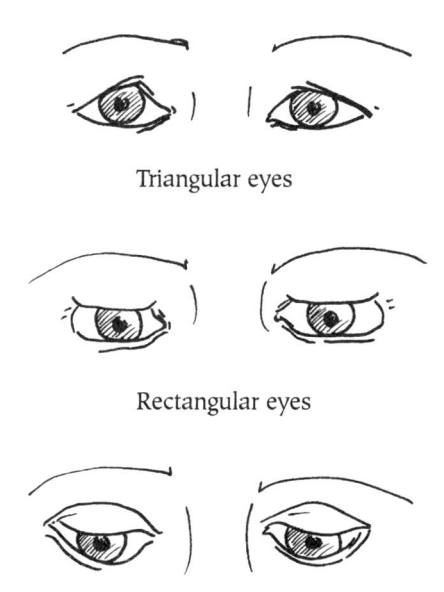

Triangular eyes

Rectangular eyes

Half-moon shaped eyes

Triangular eyes often seem as if the subject is in a state of perpetual perplexion. Such individuals seem to strike the wrong note with people in general social situations, but are able to brush away such unfortunate misapprehensions – and misapprehensions they are, because there is nothing to say that the person with triangular eyes is not noble and friendly. They do, however, have an unfortunate habit of speaking their minds, and of giving advice whether or not it has been solicited. This strange mix of ability without social grace often makes them excellent politicians – they are not afraid of getting things done, or of losing friends while they get on with it.

A rectangular eye shape is normally caused by an additional fold of skin at the top of the eye, making it look as if the subject is deep in thought – even deeper, in fact, than someone with deep-set eyes. The rectangular eye shape is a sign of someone who thinks through every aspect of their life. Fiercely intelligent, their one problem is that, unlike the person whose eyes are merely deep-set, they always run the risk of thinking too much. While others will happily throw themselves into a situation, the person with rectangular eyes will still be waiting on the sidelines, thinking through all the potential ramifications. Before they know it, the opportunity may have passed. Their desire for ultimate security and peace of mind is a two-edged sword in relationships. They may lose many perfectly suitable partners because of their own reluctance to commit, but when/if they eventually do, their choice will be totally suitable, for both persons involved.

If the eyes are shaped like half-moons, either upturned or downturned, they signify the 'cunning of the fox'. In ancient China, the fox was regarded with considerably more fear and suspicion than today in the West. Someone with fox eyes is a genius at espionage and deception, but also loyal in a curiously snobbish way. If they regard someone as their intellectual superior, they will faithfully do their bidding, but consider anyone beneath their own level as fair game for tricks and lies. Inherently skittish and cowardly, they have no stomach for fights and confrontations. Skilful manipulators of any situation for good or ill, they are the first to bolt for cover when trouble looms. They make excellent salesmen but extremely poor customer services representatives, because they are very good at starting things but extremely unwilling to risk public exposure in finishing them.

## Crossed Eyes

Crossed eyes (eyes that for whatever reason do not look in the same direction) are likely to cause the subject some embarrassment, and the end result is that they become shy. Because focusing on everyday objects involves that little bit extra of will, such people are used to expending large amounts of energy on tasks that the rest of us take for granted. Because they try just that little bit harder at everything, they are liable to be just that little bit more exact, and just that little bit better at whatever they try. However, they can also be exhausted by tasks that others might not even regard as demanding. They are susceptible to modern diseases, such as nervous exhaustion, stress and migraines, and should be careful not to try too hard.

## Eye Lashes

Short, stubby eyelashes are a symbol of someone with a short fuse. They have little to protect them from dust and flecks of sand, and their tempers can be just as quick to irritate as their eyes.

Long, curling lashes, on the other hand, keep the eye safely insulated from minor particles that might trouble it. Such protection makes the subject confident and sure of themselves, and they are constantly in search of new challenges. They can also be very forthright with their opinions – they expect everyone else to be as strong-willed as they are, and do not realize that not everyone has the luxury of such protection.

## Eye Lids

If the upper eye lids are substantially larger than the lower lids, it can give the impression that the subject is sleepy. Such people are likely to be hard to motivate. They have low expectations and rarely expect much out of life – or at least, that's what they tell themselves, as sometimes it is easier to do that than to get on with making the necessary changes.

If the lower eye lids are substantially larger than the upper eye lids, it gives the impression of a reptilian visage. Such lizard-like looks suggest a lizard-like cunning – even if such a person is your friend, beware of crocodile tears!

## Crow's feet

The lines that occasionally extend from the outer corners of the eyes are, rather disparagingly, known in the West as 'crow's feet'. On the left-hand (yang) side, each of these lines represents a person to whom the subject will be married. Old-fashioned face reading, which developed in a culture where polygamy was a popular practice, saw no problem with a man having three wives simultaneously, or indeed with a widow taking her brother-in-law as a husband to continue the family line. In modern times, these lines are more likely to represent serial marriages. They also apply to long-term 'common-law' partnerships that are marriage in all but name. However they work out in practice, each of the lines on the left-hand corners of the eyes refer to a great love or union with another human being – the deeper and longer the line, the stronger the bond.

Lines on the right-hand side of the face represent the yin (shadowy) aspect of a person's love-life – in other words the number of affairs they are likely to have. The number of lines is likely to be larger than that on the left-hand side of the face, and once again, the deeper and longer the lines are, the stronger the feelings will be between the subject and their lover.

## The tracks of tears

The subject is less lucky if they have lines that descend vertically from the base of the eyes. These look like, and are taken to signify, the tracks of tears rolling down the face, and denote a degree of suffering in later life (middle age and beyond), normally in the area of the subject's relationships. If the tracks are longer on the left-hand (yang) side, this misfortune is likely to be brought upon the subject by their own action, on the right-hand (yin) side, by their own inaction.

## CASE STUDY

You are trying to decide which of two builders you should contract to construct an extension on your home, but you cannot make up your mind between them. Builder A has up-slanting, protruding almond-shaped eyes and Builder B has small, deep-set eyes.

Builder A is shrewd and charming, but he is also likely to bite off more than he can chew. While his estimate may appear to be the most attractive, it is also the most likely to run way over budget, and he is likely to take twice as long because he's forgotten about the three other jobs he is supposed to be working on. Builder B, meanwhile, is shy and slow, but also sure. He is likely to have overestimated the price because he does not want to bring you bad news later on, and he has probably given himself the same leeway on the time he thinks it will take to complete. If you want to be pleasantly surprised by both the speed and price, you could do a lot worse than Builder B.

# The eyebrows

Chinese face reading places particular value on the eyebrows as signifiers of wisdom. The longer and bushier the eyebrows, the more a subject is said to look like the great sages Confucius or Lao Zi.

The brows are also seen as a good signifier of one's emotional state. They are an important part of non-verbal communication, often inadvertent, and can be so easy to read that in ancient times it was the practice of court ladies to shave their eyebrows off to avoid giving their secret feelings away.

## Thickness of the brow

Thick, chunky eyebrows are a symbol of a warm heart and a generous nature. Such people love life, always enjoy themselves and never at the expense of others. Happy-go-lucky is perhaps the best way to describe them, with emphasis on the 'happy' and the 'lucky'. They may not be rich, but they never want for anything. The darker the brows, the healthier a life they can expect to lead. Such eyebrows are often unpopular with women, who pluck them to reduce their apparent size – but this has little effect on their good fortune. The large brows are still there under the surface.

Thin, attenuated brows are a sign of someone who prizes organization and order above all things. There is not necessarily anything wrong with this, but the owner of thin brows is likely to prefer the order in question to be organized by other people. Instead of facing life head on, the owner of thin brows hopes that solutions will present themselves as if by magic. Much of the troubles that afflict them can, eventually, be traced back to their own refusal to get involved at crucial moments.

## Distance between brows

Brows that are close together can often make the subject appear as if they are scowling in intense concentration. Intensity is the watchword here – this person fully believes that they can achieve anything if they put their mind to it. Obviously, this has its good and bad points. They are not afraid to try anything once, but in some areas, especially the work place, they may often find themselves biting off more than they can chew. In affairs of the heart, their dogged refusal to give up makes them persistent and insistent suitors – they will not take no for an answer, even when it is as clear as day to everyone else. In relationships they can be jealous and aggressive – their refusal to listen to reason can, if left unchecked, lead them to see infidelities where there are none, and end up causing more strife than resolution.

Unlike the close-browed, their opposite numbers with wide-spaced eyebrows are eternally hesitant. They prefer to let others make decisions and take the lead – it is not that they don't want to be the centre of attention or the leader of the gang, just that they have very little confidence in their own abilities. Hen-pecked husbands and passive wives can expect to have this kind of eyebrow, if, that is, they ever overcome their shyness to actually speak to a member of the opposite sex.

Some eyebrows, of course, have no distance between them because they meet in the middle. Such joined brows are a sign of hypersensitivity – the subject is liable to take chance comments personally, hold grudges and do a very good job of making acquaintances feel guilty, even if the slights are only imaginary. This tendency for emotional bruising has obvious effects on the love life, but relationships influence joined-brow people in a slightly different way. A man with joined brows may be successful in the workplace, but to really succeed he needs an ever-supportive wife. The stresses of working life will only wash over him for as long as he can go home to someone who can smooth all his worries away.

Conversely, a woman with joined brows is likely to find her hypersensitivity manifesting itself in a heightened awareness of her biological clock. No matter how well she may be doing in her career, she will jump at the chance to get out and make a home and babies. She will see it as a chance to avoid the stresses of the workplace, but is likely to discover that home life merely brings with it new worries.

## Shapes

Face reading lists a vast number of variants in eyebrow shape, but the following are the ones you are most likely to encounter. If the eyebrows are shaped like new-moons, with an elegant, rounded curve, it is a sign of a lunar changeability. This person's personality will be as ever-changing as the phases of the moon, but also just as predictable for those that know them. In relationships they are helplessly sexual, often rating sexual prowess above any other quality in a potential mate. They also flourish in the presence of a 'sun' whose light they can reflect – such people work best in careers that require someone else's efforts – for example, as actors (who require someone else's script), musicians (who require someone else's music), or salesmen (who require someone else's product).

Triangular eyebrows

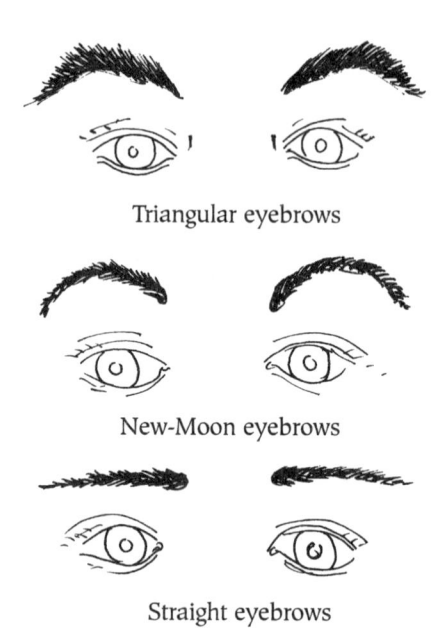

New-Moon eyebrows

Straight eyebrows

If the brows are pointed to the extent of looking almost triangular, this is a powerful symbol of the Fire element, and hence of vigour and passion. They take everything to extremes, and unless sternly controlled by others, are likely to eat up everything like a raging furnace. This can apply in all walks of life – in the workplace they may place excessive demands on their fellow workers, in friendships they may be all take and no give, and in relationships likewise. However, such all-engulfing heat has its bonuses: many will find them irresistibly charming, and will happily succumb to their flaming passions, even at the risk of getting burned. Women with triangular eyebrows are less likely to be so passionate – the flames may make them emotional, but they will also dry their ardour, making them sociable but not necessarily passionate.

Chaotic unruly eyebrows with no discernible shape are a signifier of equally haphazard organizational skills. These people have trouble marshalling their thoughts and their deeds in all aspects of their fate, which can make them clumsy and even inadvertently tactless.

In relationships, men with this eyebrow type benefit immensely from a sensible, well-organized partner, though they themselves may prove to be endlessly exasperating too.

Similarly, the owner of eyebrows with noticeably curly hair tend to approach other aspects of their fate in a circular manner. They are adept at coming up with new ideas, although exactly how useful they turn out to be is open to debate. They are also often obsessed with themselves to the point of narcissism. The curly-browed man risks a lonely love life through his refusal to settle with one particular person. The curly-browed woman is not quite so prone to overt egotism, since she often projects her own desire for success onto her partner.

Straight eyebrows that sit above the eyes in horizontal lines, are thought to represent someone with a straight, perhaps even narrow mind. They are skilled at making money – the eyebrows resemble the Chinese numeral '1', and this makes the subject good at mathematics. They are good-natured and good-humoured, but often strive to be no more than average. They are often best described as 'average' – whatever survey or statistics you consult, the people who cluster in the middle of the bell curve will be the ones with straight eyebrows. They are often straightforward and mundane, neither striving for extreme power nor falling far behind into penury. In relationships, they are as predictable as in other areas of life, often conforming to traditional stereotypes. Straight-browed men like to play the field, while straight-browed women are dead-set on marriage and a home – neither are particularly acrobatic in bed.

Very short eyebrows that barely form a covering over the top of the eye are a symbol of someone without much of a 'roof' over their emotional head. They are easily hurt and almost totally given to their emotions – they have very strong passions, and cannot control them easily. In relationships they can be brutally selfish, but if they fall in love it will be earth-moving stuff.

## Height of Eyebrows

If the eyebrows are set particularly low over the eyes, the person appears to be concentrating intensely on whatever is in front of them.

The key word with such a person is focus – on anything and everything. They are slaves to ambition, voraciously curious about the world and the people around them, and hypnotically persuasive – they make great scientists. However, without a position of power or some authority, they can become interfering busybodies – remember to check other facial features to see how they interact with others.

Brows that sit relatively high on the forehead are a sign of someone in a permanent state of surprise. This is not necessarily a bad thing – they can be permanently surprised by their own good fortune and incredible luck. Whatever the positive or negative aspects of their fate, they are often liable to be passive participants in it. This is the person who is surprised by their inheritance, by their lucky finds or by their chance meetings that bring them ever greater luck. Luck is the key word here, though it could just as easily be their surprise at their incredibly bad fortune that brings them that startled look.

## Sloping

The best kind of eyebrow to have in Chinese face reading is the upward-sloping or 'dragon' brow. Although they may appear placid and meek, people with such features are long-term planners with powerful personalities and great resolve. They can literally put their minds to anything, and they have the blessings of the fates for any task they attempt. Dragon brows are most likely to be found on leaders, but they are not perfect – they are apt to leave many tasks unfinished, and are easily bored by subjects or situations, or even people that do not hold their interest.

If the eyebrows slope downwards, the subject looks as if they are living in a constant state of frustration. Good fortune does come to such individuals, but only after a great deal of hard work. They are honest, perhaps too honest for their own good, and fated to have the permanent look of the harassed shopkeeper. Success normally comes late in life to these types, since it normally takes them at least until their late thirties before they are in any position to start working for themselves in building up their own fortune.

## Minor Eyebrow Features

If the inner ends of the eyebrows come to a point while the outer ends are much fatter, giving the overall impression of two comets going in different directions, the subject is said to be indecisive. They are eternally looking for someone who can make their decisions for them, resulting in both sexes in a desire for early marriage and family. In a family situation, they can make wonderful parents, as long as their other half is not similarly browed.

If the inner ends of the eyebrow shoot up vertically, it is a symptom of a tough childhood. This is not necessarily a bad thing – the subject's life may have been changed immeasurably for the better by being forced to work hard at an early age. These people are eager to please and hard-working, with the only obvious downside being that, after a while, they will expect fate to reward them for their efforts. By the time they reach their thirties, they may feel hard-done-by – like the children they once were, they are still waiting for a parental figure to pat them on the head and congratulate them for a job well-done, but the praise is not always forthcoming. Such feelings can make them bitter and resentful to the world that they feel has wronged them. Their behaviour in relationships will depend on which part of this cycle you catch them. Their eagerness to satisfy their partner's every desire can turn them into accomplished and skilful bedroom athletes – but beware: unless you think you can become the reward they are looking for, do not play around with their feelings.

If the hairs of the brow curve downwards, it is a sign of someone who may always aim high, but will often find themselves falling short. They may often develop a negative attitude towards life, but their very introspection often makes them accomplished creatives.

One eyebrow higher than the other is a sign of overdeveloped facial muscles in one side of the face. It is perhaps one of the most obvious examples of that age-old maxim 'don't make that face or you'll get stuck with it'. If the subject consistently makes arch comments, snootily dismissing others with a single raised eyebrow, over time it will build up into this very feature – the arms and legs are not the only muscles that bulk up with exercise! One raised eyebrow will often signify an arch, intemperate character, overly critical of others but also of themselves, with a sense of tradition and history that often manifests itself through a snobbish hatred of the new. Beneath the imperious surface, however, lurks a soul that is easily bruised – these people can rarely take criticism as readily as they dish it out. They often have few friends, because they can be vicious in answering imagined slights that were only meant in jest. By the time they realize that they overreacted, another friend has left them never to return.

## Broken

If there is a gap in the eyebrow, this is generally regarded in an unfavourable light by face readers, chiefly because the reasons for its appearance are universally linked to bad fortune. Perhaps the subject has a habit of tugging absent-mindedly on their brows while thinking – a sign of stress that will pay off with a bald spot if their eyebrow hair (like many people's) doesn't grow back once plucked. Perhaps the gap in the brow is there because of a scar – an old war wound perhaps, or the result of a childhood accident. Either way, the scars are signs of strife and trouble in the subject's life, and just because they are old, it does not necessarily mean that the subject has lost their ability to get into fights, fall off logs or not dodge an incoming bullet. Those with broken brows are apt to hold grudges for a long time, and are often prone to disaster. Even if their life remains relatively trouble-free, they will constantly work under the belief that only stressing and fretting keeps everything from going completely wrong.

## Brow Lines

If a single vertical line appears between your eyebrows when you frown, this is a sign that something is worrying you. You may not even be aware of it, but something at the back of your mind is pressing its way to the front, making a little dent in your face as it goes. If you see this mark on someone else, you'll know that they have something weighing on their mind, and may need some help or advice.

If two vertical lines appear in the space between your eyebrows whenever you frown, this is a good sign. To the Chinese, this shows that you concentrate hard when it matters, and do not take your eyes off your aims and objectives. It is a sign that you can make your own good fortune, because you are not a quitter.

If you have three vertical lines in between your brows instead of two, this is a sign of supreme concentration and supreme success. Consider a career as a professional chess player, bomb disposal expert or circus knife-thrower. You may not think that you have what it takes, but when you set your mind on something you are harder to shake off than an angry shark.

Watch out, however, if you have more than three vertical lines in between your brows. It is possible to have too much of a good thing, and if your brows spend all their time furrowed in intense concentration on the tiniest details, you will eventually blow a fuse. If you have too many lines in between your brows, you also have too many troubles. Calm down, have a nice cup of tea, and try and reduce your workload.

## CASE STUDY

You are organizing a big charity event and you need to decide who is going to be on the door to take the money. Mr A has straight, downward-pointing eyebrows with a single line that appears in between them when he frowns. He does not seem too keen on doing the job, but he says he'll do it if nobody else is interested. Ms B, on the other hand, has been getting ready all week for her big moment. She has delicate, thin, curved eyebrows with a double-line between them when she frowns. Who should you choose?

Mr A is your man, because although he is not that bothered about the task, you know he will do a good job and will not let you down. Give him something to do and he will make sure it is done properly. Ms B is simply looking forward to the social aspect of the job and will be useless with the money. She is likely to get bored after a few minutes and desert her post.

# 5 Cheeks, Jaw and Chin

*Bones are the most difficult part of the face to read, because you need to touch a face, not watch from a distance. They are also very easy to obscure, for both men and women. Men can grow beards to hide their jaw and chin, and even a day's growth can create so much shadow it becomes very difficult to see the important features. Women, of course, can wear make-up, which adds shading to the contours of the face.*

## Cheeks

The Chinese say that a sensitive person has 'thin cheeks', because they are quick to change colour – rosy when they are out in the cool, fresh air, and bright red when they are embarrassed. Similarly, if someone has no shame, or never gives others any sign of what they are really thinking, the Chinese say that they have 'thick cheeks'.

With the permanent bones that underlie the cheeks, however, there is a different story. You should be able to feel two nobbly bits under the skin – these are the bones that determine a person's powers of leadership. Natural-born leaders have prominent cheek-bones, like twin mountains on their face, demonstrating their ability to weigh the facts in any situation and decide the right course of action.

A person with high, distinctive cheek-bones has a commanding presence and people will always stop and listen to them. This does not necessarily mean they are saying the right things – cheek-bones are all about charisma, not intelligence. Before you start following the orders of someone with this kind of profile, remember to check the rest of their face to see if they really are someone you can trust.

If someone has narrow cheek-bones, very close to the nose, their mind, like their face, can tend to be a little narrow. They may be blinkered in their outlook, suffer from tunnel vision or ignore the ideas of others. As leaders, they have trouble adapting to new situations. You can trust them to guide their friends to a specific goal, but if plans change they will have no idea what to do next.

Flat cheek-bones that hardly stick out at all suggests someone who is not interested in sticking out themselves. They could be a general in the army or an admiral in the fleet, but with flat cheek-bones they will not feel like leading anyone anywhere, and nobody would listen to them if they tried. Flat cheek-bones are a sign of an easy-going, carefree character. If you have to deal with someone with flat cheek-bones, you'll get more done by talking to their assistant, because that will be the person who makes the decisions.

# Jaw

The jaw is another important part of the face's bone structure, and its shape is also related to leadership and dealings with others. While the cheeks tell us about the likelihood of others listening to what you have to say, the jaw tells us more about why you might want to order them around in the first place.

A normal jaw line is the same breadth as the forehead. Measure it by holding up your hands to the part of your forehead where your hair begins, and, keeping your hands at right angles to the ground, see if you naturally touch the bottom of your jaw. If your jaw is this broad, and rounded too, then your intentions will always be honourable.

If the jaw is broad but squarer, then it is a sign of pride and devotion to duty. A square-jawed person will always work hard and strive for perfection, but risks being too stubborn. Like a dogged war hero, they will always be leading the battle charge right through enemy lines, whether or not there is really an enemy to charge towards. These people need to be kept active and busy, otherwise they will start rustling up trouble as they try to find something to do.

If the jaw is so broad that it is actually wider than the forehead, the owner is a real fighter, and may even be a bit of a bully. They always expect to get their own way, and normally do. They are as hard as nails when driving any sort of bargain, and they are natural leaders. If anyone stands up to them, they are liable to take it personally, so watch out. The best way to avoid getting into trouble with them is not to put yourself in a position where they give you an order. That way, you will not have to refuse them and hurt their feelings.

If the jaw is rounded and smooth, not square at all, it is a sign that power is unimportant to the owner. They may well occupy a position of authority, but they will be doing the job because they want to, or because it needs to be done, or even because they inherited it from somebody else. The one thing you can guarantee is that they will not be doing the job because they enjoy being in charge, because they do not. The person who has a rounded jaw has nothing to prove. If they see two people having a heated argument they will just walk on by without a second thought, because they cannot think of anything on the planet that is really worth fighting about. They have the same attitude towards one-upmanship. You will never see someone with a rounded jaw back-stabbing their way to the top of the class or the head of the company – they are simply not interested in competition. The downside is that they can sometimes be complacent. Since they have no desire to get involved in contests, they sometimes find themselves left at the sidelines. While it can be quite noble not to worry about who wins a race, if everybody acted like this there would be no races at all, no competition, no games, no sport, and no progress. There are two sides to everything.

## Oval face

If the jaw goes down towards a point, it will make the face look oval. This, according to the Chinese, is a good thing – the oval face is a sign of true beauty. There can be a negative side, with regards to power. Because many people are easily persuaded by a pretty face, beautiful people tend to get their own way a lot of the time. Queues, pedestrian crossings, traffic lights, all these things mean nothing to those blessed with good looks – everybody seems to want to help them. Just as knights used to place cloaks on the ground for their ladies to walk on, pretty people are feted everywhere they go, and they sometimes start to expect people to do whatever they tell them. For this reason, the face reading for a slightly pointed jaw (making an oval face) shows that the subject can expect an easy time of it when they are young, but nobody remains young and beautiful forever. The time will come, even for little angels, when they cannot get away with fluttering their eyelashes any more – it can be quite a rude awakening.

Suddenly, they cannot get to the front of the queue any more, and the lead role in the play is taken by somebody younger and better looking. Having an easy time is not a good face fortune for the Chinese, because they know that winter will always follow summer. People cannot get by on looks alone; they must store something for the cold months ahead as they enter the autumn of their lives. The things that must be stored for your future good fortune are friendships, favours, love and knowledge. If you are too busy admiring your own reflection and waiting for fans to bring you food and finish your work for you, you could be in for a nasty surprise.

## Pointed face

If the jaw is very pointed, the entire face appears to be narrow, even triangular or a little wedge-shaped. The further such a person goes on life's path, the less space they will have to walk in. It is as if they are walking along a pretty mountain trail, that slowly gets thinner and thinner until they are teetering across a knife-edge between two sheer drops. These people never quite reach their goals, and always get bogged down in something else that keeps them from getting where they really want to go. This is not quite as bad as it sounds. Just as having a pretty face can actually be bad news to the Chinese, because it encourages you to take others for granted, never reaching your ultimate goal can actually be quite a good thing. The trick is, say the Chinese, always to aim high – stupidly high. Make sure that your goals in life are way, way above other people's; it cannot hurt to have a shot at the moon, and you know that you will never find yourself on a downhill streak. For someone fated never to hit the ultimate high, it is quite possible that their life will consist of success after success. You will not find them peaking early on and falling into despair. Just be advised that whatever they tell you they are aiming for, they will not actually get.

# Chin

Although you may think they are one and the same, the chin and jaw are separate entities. The jaw may slope and curve leisurely towards the chin, only to suddenly jut out squarely. Similarly, you might have a blocky jaw, only to end in a fat, rounded double chin. However, in most cases, the chin will be a predictable continuation of the jaw itself: a square jaw is most likely to finish up with an equally-square chin; a rounded jaw will probably round itself off nicely with a rounded chin. In this case, the face reading for the chin merely repeats what the jaw reading has already told you. Nevertheless, if you are feeling a little unsure about the jaw, the chin ought to set your mind at rest. If the two readings for chin and jaw are the complete opposite of each other, the simple answer is that they cancel each other out.

Just as with the jaw, if a chin is square it is a sign that the owner is bold, brash and impulsive. Like a boxer in the middle of a big fight, they will not be afraid of taking it on the chin, but they also stand the risk of getting a little punch-drunk. They might be good in a fight, be it a real-life fight, a fight of idea or a fight for attention or success. Sometimes they may go looking for trouble. Someone with this kind of chin is great in powerful struggles, such as sporting contests, but you would not want them as a bodyguard – they might keep you safe, but if they could not find anyone suspicious they would start picking fights with everybody else.

Pointed chin

Broad chin

Square chin

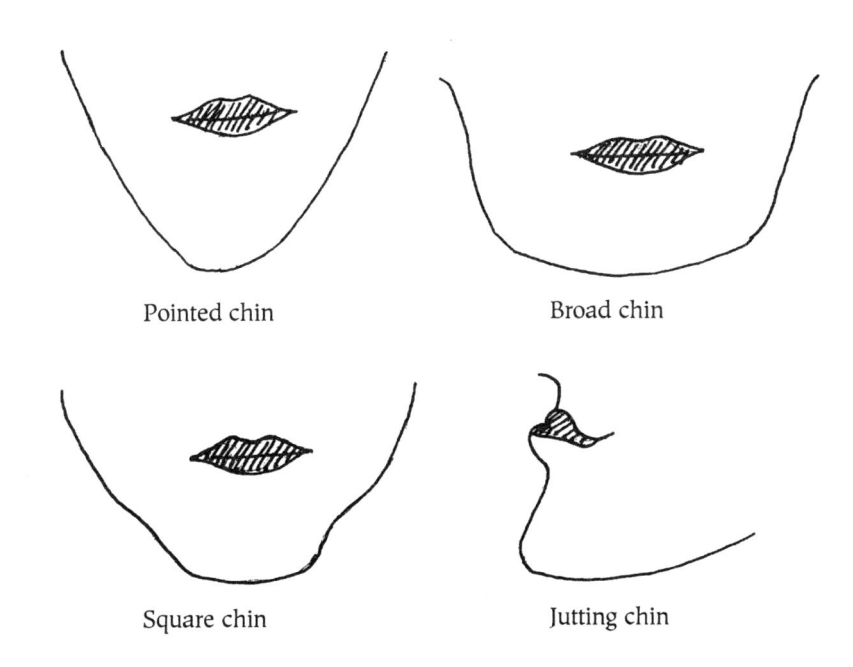

Jutting chin

If someone has a pointed chin, making their head look as if it is shaped like a kite, then their fortune is likely to be blown by the winds of fate. This kind of person is blinkered and indecisive. Their decisions will change and change again as they are blown from all directions by all kinds of breeze. They will have an excuse for everything, but after a while, their friends will realize that they never stop. They will always be late (for a perfectly good reason, of course), forget important meetings (or have to cancel) and the chances of them ever handing in their assignments on time is almost zero. However, like the kite itself, these people will not realize that they are being buffeted by forces beyond their control. They may think they are as free as a bird, but someone far away is holding their strings and tugging them in different directions. If you know somebody like this, look carefully to see if there is a powerful, domineering family member behind the scenes. Like Cinderella, they may have a strict parent or ugly sisters in the background, forcing them to slave away all day doing everybody else's chores. If you ever visit the house and the owner of the pointed chin makes a show of lazing around, look very carefully. You may find that they have been working for hours to make it look as if they do no work at all.

If the chin is very long and very pointed, so long in fact that it seems to enter a room before the owner does, the owner may be someone who enjoys interfering in other people's affairs. We may sometimes say that someone is 'nosy', but Chinese noses very rarely grow so long that anyone would talk of someone 'sticking their noses into other people's business'. Instead, it is the big chin that is a sign of interference, and the chin that is a sign of a gossipy nature. Be careful what you tell this person because, true or false, it is likely to be broadcast from the rooftops before you know it.

You are much better off if you confide your secrets in someone with a rounded chin that does not stick out at all. Just as a rounded jaw is a sign of someone with nothing to prove, a rounded chin completes the picture. If the chin is not prominent, then you are looking at someone who doesn't like to take risks or play power games. They do not mind who has the upper hand so long as they are making a good job of it. This makes them very diplomatic, because they care about other people's feelings. Your secrets are safe with them.

If the chin is a double-chin, or even a triple or a quadruple, the subject has a few excess pounds on their frame. The chances are high that they are lazy or unsporty, and prefer to vegetate in front of the television all day.

## Chin profiles

You do not just have to look at a chin from the front – the profile view will show you how far it sticks out. If the chin sticks out like a little ramp at the front of the face, then this is yet another sign of someone who likes getting into trouble, and sticking their nose (or chin) where it does not belong.

On the other hand, if the chin is not there at all (if the front of the face just seems to curve back from the lower lip towards the neck), this person might start with big ideas, but they are easily discouraged. While their big-chinned companions will rush right in, the 'chinless wonder' will vacillate and prevaricate. However bold they may talk, they have a deep, dark secret, which is that they are really very timid and cannot bear the thought of getting into trouble. They do not like positions of responsibility, and instead prefer to be left alone. They will leave others alone in turn. This kind of person would work well in a library – you can guarantee they will get on with their work quietly. The only drawback would come if anyone else ever caused a disturbance, because the chinless wonder would not want to start any trouble by asking them to shut up or get out.

## CASE STUDY

There is no alternative – someone is going to have to talk to your child's teacher about the way she is running the class. You and the other parents have all agreed, but who is the best person to send in as an envoy? This is a job that requires tact and patience – the various components of the face should all interact with one another to produce a whole, but for the sake of argument, we will just concentrate on what we can learn from the chin. Ms A has a broad jaw but narrow cheeks – she would be bold and unstoppable, but simply will not listen to reason, and you want to give the teacher a chance to explain herself. Mrs B has a pointed chin and high, distinctive cheekbones, which should make him a commanding presence, but not one who will necessarily be able to act on the information he receives. However, the person who should really go is Mrs C, who has both high cheekbones, a jaw that is broader at the ears and the round chin of a diplomat.

# 6 YIN AND YANG

*The first half of this book lists the elements of face reading that are easiest to quantify. Face reading in this way may be fun, but it is still a very basic form of the ancient art. Just as astrology cannot be reasonably expected to predict the daily lives of an entire twelfth of the population in a given stroke, nor should such simplistic definitions of face reading be expected to bring genuinely exacting results.*

We have already seen how combinations of readings of different parts of the face can alter and focus our perception of the subject's face and fate, but there is still more. The most important aspect of face reading that we have yet to tackle is the subject's inherent active or passive attitude towards the world in different aspects of their fate.

## Yin and Yang

Chinese philosophy divides the universe into two striving forces, yin and yang. Neither can exist without the other. They are essential components in any object, and perfection can only be achieved when both are perfectly balanced. The yin-yang symbol is well known all over the world, showing light and dark eternally circling each other, the two halves making a unifying circle, and each containing a tiny dot of the other at its centre. Calling these forces good and evil, or positive and negative, is a poor translation, since a well-rounded individual cannot exist without having an element of both – which is why this book, even though it strives to keep Chinese terminology to a minimum, has left these terms untranslated.

Chinese thought recognizes such a thing as destiny, but also that human beings have free will. Fate may install certain predispositions in someone's life, but we all have the right to try and alter the hand that we have been dealt. Only someone with perfectly balanced features could ever be said to have wishes and desires that are in perfect keeping with the predictions made by astrologers at the time of their birth. For the rest of us, we have the chance to go our own way, for good or ill.

## Yin and Yang in Face Reading

We divide the body's yin and yang influences with a line down the centre of the face. Everything on the right side is in the yin area, and everything on the left side is yang. Yin features denote those aspects of the subject's fate that are determined by their own passivity – in other words, what is done to and for them by others. The right side tells us much about the person's family, genetic predispositions and treatment by others.

Yang features, meanwhile, tell us about those areas of fortune that are determined by a person's own activity – in other words, what they themselves do to and for others. The left side tells us about the person's own will, decisions and behaviour towards others. So each of the 'double' features of the face (the eyes, brows and ears), not only informs us about a particular area of fate (just as the nose denotes wealth and the mouth emotion) but also allows us to be much more exact about exactly how that fate will work out.

Most people have features that are slightly uneven, and it is in the difference between the two sides of the face that we can pinpoint their role in their own fortune.

# Yin aspects

The right-hand side of the face is the 'yin' side, associated with passivity and the influence of others. If the features on this side are larger or more prominent than on the other, then the subject is apt to be influenced, pushed, bullied or persuaded by others. It is also the side of the face that emphasizes intellect and emotions.

> ### CASE STUDY
>
> You notice that your subject's right nostril is almost imperceptibly larger than their left. Knowing that the nostrils influence the amount of spending, and that a yin imbalance emphasizes the influence of others, what does this tell you about their spending habits? Are they the sort of person who readily comes up with the cash, or do they have to be cajoled into buying a round of drinks?

## Yang aspects

The left-hand side of the face is the 'yang' side, associated with activity and the subject's assertion of their own demands. If the features on this side are larger or more prominent than on the other, then the subject is more likely to have an influence over others. Such a person is more likely to make decisions on another's behalf, and is most likely to take the lead in any situation. In terms of face reading, it will mean that the feature in question, and the area of fate that it rules, will be more likely to be tied up in decisions made *by* the subject, not *for* them.

> ### CASE STUDY
>
> A subject has one eyebrow slightly larger than the other, and you see that it is clearly not just a case of a greater amount of hair/hair follicles, but also partly due to more developed muscles on that side of the face. The single raised eyebrow is a sign of an arch refusal to be impressed with others. If it is overdeveloped on the yang (left) side, it is a sign that the subject is rarely moved by the efforts of others because they feel they can do better. The chances are very high that they will go on to do so, just to prove that their way is better. If it is overdeveloped on the yin (right) side, it is more likely to be a defensive reaction to others' superior talents – i.e., an attempt to hide their own feelings of inadequacy, as they feel put-upon by the successes of their fellows.

# TRANSIENT FEATURES

*Facial features, separately and in combination, added to the positive–negative readings afforded by yin and yang sides, can create a very detailed and personalized face reading. With these tools, you should be able to demonstrate quite accurate knowledge of someone's overall fate and character, but the focus will still not be sharp. You will be able to tell someone about the long-term, general direction of their life, but less about the immediate here and now. This is because the face, like the hand in palmistry, is a map of the whole life, and consequently retains much information covering several decades.*

For pinpoint accuracy about moments in the present time, plus or minus a few weeks, we must turn to the transient features of the face. Although almost every aspect of the human face can be altered by the passage of time, skin features such as moles, spots, cold sores, blemishes and scars can come and go. These features also rarely appear in symmetrical pairs, and so their presence allows for much more personalized readings. Moles are often permanent parts of the face, though their fluctuation in size may cause changes in apparent fortune over time. Spots and scars are very much readings of the moment. A spot that develops soon before or after someone makes a decision, may well appear on a part of the face that rules a particular aspect of their life. It may appear in a positive or negative light, or even in a sector of the face that seems completely inconsequential, leading to a prediction of future events that would otherwise be thought of as unrelated.

# The Mark of Worry

A mole or birthmark on the very top of the forehead, bordering on the hairline itself, is a symbol of stress and worry. If it is something the owner regularly finds themselves playing with or scratching absent-mindedly, it sets up a feedback loop of head-scratching, and if the subject is not careful, acting out the motions of concern will eventually lead to them finding more things to be concerned about.

On the right-hand (yin) side of the forehead, this mark denotes a passive fate – the subject's worries will stem from their own inactivity. Jobs left undone or never even started, tardiness caused by oversleeping or perhaps even an inability to grasp the nettle and have a good row with a recalcitrant spouse – all these things are likely to be the roots of troubles for the owner of a yin worry, and all of them are ultimately the result of some form of passivity.

On the left-hand (yang) side of the forehead, this mark denotes an active fate. The owner will still be constantly worried, but the problems are likely to originate from their own activity. They will take on more work than they can reasonably be expected to handle; they will turn up for work too early and find themselves without a key to get in, or in relationships they may prove to be overbearing or speak out of turn.

# The Mark of Intellect

A mole or birthmark in the middle of the forehead is a sign of a great mind. On the left-hand (yang) side this will be a result of active involvement – for example, a hard-working, active student. On the right-hand (yin) side it will be largely thanks to good teachers and schooling. Either way, the subject will have a powerful mind. A supreme intellect is signified by a mole on the temple, with the same proviso for yin and yang influences.

Someone with a yang mark of intellect is likely to make a good teacher, because they take an active interest in disseminating their knowledge to the world. Someone with a yin mark will be less likely to enjoy imparting lessons to students – they are more likely to be solitary researchers.

There is a price to be paid, however, such a mole may also have an adverse influence on the subject's love life. While they remain buried in their books and getting dusty in underground archives, they may be losing out socially. If the mark is still in the middle of the forehead but on the right-hand (yin) side, the subject's love fortune will simply not have the chance to flourish. They risk being forever the shy wallflower, nose in a book while others around them pair off and settle down. They left-hand (yang) variant is perhaps even more tragic, because it implies that the subjects' active interest in their studies will actually keep them too busy. They may well find themselves in the company of the perfect partner, but will turn down any offers of romance because they are too preoccupied with other things. One day, they may have cause to regret such a blasé attitude towards affairs of the heart.

# The Mark of Travel

A mole or birthmark between the eyebrow and the temple resembles for the Chinese a pointer inviting the eye to wander, and the end result is a predisposition to travel. If the mark is permanent, it will be a constant desire to move on to new pastures, with settling down a virtual impossibility. If the mark is caused by a transient mark, such as a spot, it is a sign that travel is looming in the subject's fate – perhaps a holiday, or a move occasioned by a change of career. The side of the face will determine how the subject's own decisions influence this wanderlust. If the mark occurs on the left (yang) side, it will be their own willpower that drives them ever onwards. They will be inveterate travellers, always keen to seek out new places and new experiences. If the mark occurs on the right (yin) side, they may even be the kind of person who hates travelling or holidays, but will constantly find themselves being passively whisked away to foreign climates.

## The Mark of the 'Third Eye'

A mole or birthmark between the eyebrows looks like a 'third eye', and is a sign of someone who can see things that others cannot. They are likely to be dreamers and thinkers, often very perceptive about others' problems, but given to depression because they are unable to solve their own. Some form of spiritual ability is also possible – a mark that is closer to the left (yang) side denotes an individual with a certain charismatic power over others, actively able to influence them. A mark that is closer to the right (yin) side suggests someone with a passive kind of spirituality – perhaps a sense of clairvoyance or prophecy.

Other schools of face reading regard this mark more simply, as a sign of supreme luck. For them, it signifies a pearl suspended mid-air between 'twin dragons' (the eyebrows). The subject can expect excellent fortune and may expect to lead a charmed life.

## The Mark of Tears

A mole or birthmark between the eye and the nose is said to be in the path of tears, and doomed forever to be watered by them. Women in particular with this feature are supposed to risk a melancholy and unsatisfying love life. A woman with a right (yin) weeping mole risks being eternally dumped in favour of others, or always finding herself with partners who do not seem to be ideal. A woman with a left (yang) mole, however, is an active participant in her own misery. She may be permanently in search of someone better, she may be too demanding, or she may simply scare off potential partners – however it happens, the end result will be the same. Although this is supposed to be a female trait in the Chinese face reading manuals, the author sees to reason why this feature should not apply to men with equal force.

## The Mark of Power

A mole or birthmark high on the cheek bones is a commanding presence – literally. It draws in the gaze of others, but keeps their eyes trained deferentially just below the line of sight of the subject. The owner of such a mark is used to giving orders and having others obey them; they are a born leader and always keep their head in a crisis. They are also given to bouts of melancholy, for such is the loneliness of command. While they may often find themselves at the head of the table or at the front of the group, their ability to run organizations does not necessarily cross over into friendships and relationships. These people risk losing friends and lovers by being too demanding, and should always remember that there are some situations that don't call for leaders, but listeners.

If the mark is on the right (yin) side of the face, their destiny is tied up with leadership as a passive phenomenon. Positions of responsibility will fall into their laps whether they like it or not. They might even be the leader who begs to be relieved of the burden of command – the future Emperor found cowering behind the curtains because he can think of nothing so terrible as taking over the reins of power.

If the mark is on the left (yang) side of the face, the subject's destiny is concerned with leadership as an active phenomenon. They will hunger after power with a real energy, will seek it out in whatever situation they find themselves, even clambering over others to get it. If the subject does not watch out, they may find themselves becoming the ultimate Machiavellian schemer – they might well not see a problem with this, but their friends might...

## The Mark of Friendship

A mole or birthmark further down the cheek, on the flesh of the cheek proper rather than the bony ridge of its upper reaches, it is the sign of a truly sociable individual. Such 'beauty spots' encourage the subject to get out there and meet people. They are excellent networkers and understanding friends. Friends are of paramount importance to the person with this kind of mark, often at the expense of their actual family, who will often wonder if there could not have been a mix-up at the hospital. The subject is likely to be the archetypal child who leaves their small town behind them for a glamorous life in the city, never to write home.

If the mark is on the left (yang) side, the subject has an active interest in the wild social whirl they find themselves within. A few quiet contemplative moments indoors with the relatives, and they will be itching to sneak down the drainpipe and off to the nearest party. If they are uninvited guests, they will crash the gathering anyway, and hope their winning charm will carry them through – most of the time, it will.

If the mark is on the right (yin) side, the subject's socialite existence will be caused by passive influences. Their negative relationship with their family may drive them to seek the comfort of others. Conversely, their family may be completely blameless, but may be set up by manipulative 'friends' as a stuffy, ignorant influence to be subverted at every opportunity. Someone with a yin mark of friendship risks becoming the archetypal rebellious teenager, permanently getting into parental arguments because of their attitude – whether or not their teen years are far behind them!

# The Mark of Prosperity

The nose is, as we have already seen, tied up with wealth, and a mole or birthmark there will be an indicator of financial good fortune. On the left (yang) side it will be a sign of business acumen, of an uncanny ability to close the right deals and make the right investments. On the right (yin) side, the subject's good fortune will be more passive – they are likely to inherit vast sums from distant aunts they hardly knew, find enormous bank errors in their favour or discover bags of money lying in the street with nobody to see what happens next.

If, however, the mark is on the very tip of the nose, it is a sign that financial life will not all be plain sailing. Whatever prosperity the subject enjoys, they should always be wary of any influences that are likely to undermine it. It may be undeniable that they are skilled at making money – but hanging onto it may be another matter. The chances are high indeed that the financial ups and downs are themselves brought by happy events – this mark is associated in many schools of face reading with fertility. A subject bearing such a mark is fated to have many children, and may often find that carefully planned budgets have to be swiftly rewritten to accommodate the arrival of another bundle of joy.

# The Mark of Family

Moles or birthmarks on the ears are also signs of prosperity, but of a family nature. One or more of these marks on the ears will bring success to the house and home, and whatever troubles the subject experiences in other areas of their fate, their family life will always remain safely intact.

A mole on the left-hand (yang) side will make the subject an active pursuer of family fortune. They may be adept at wooing their perfect spouse – quite different from being a skilful charmer and flirt – someone with this mark plays for keeps or not at all. They will always be ready with a tool-kit to keep the family home in perfect shape, or perhaps they will simply place their family first in all matters and ensure that nothing ever forces them into a position where they have to leave their spouse or children in the lurch.

A mole on the right-hand (yin) side is the mark of passive success in family matters. Their perfect spouse might walk right up and introduce themselves without them expanding any effort. They might win a competition for the ideal home to save themselves actually buying one, or they may simply find that others are always on hand to smooth the path of their marital difficulties.

The only downside of this mark is that it will affect non-familial areas of the subject's fortune. Unless such marks also appear in career areas of their face, they can expect their home life to impinge on their work. They will be happy and prosperous, and enjoy the uncountable riches of a loving family, but their rank in the company and their chances of becoming the head of a large company are small. Family comes first, at the expense of everything else, and this may also include friends. Owners of this mark should take care that they do not alienate their single friends with endless tales of child-rearing and marital subjects – they should remember that many people will not be interested, mostly because deep-down it makes them very jealous.

# The Mark of Sensuality

A mole or birthmark on or around the mouth is a mark of sensuality. In daily life, this will manifest itself as a discerning interest in fine wines and good foods – such a person will develop sophisticated gourmet tastes at an early age.

If the mark is on the left (yang) side, the subject will actively seek new sensual experiences, hunting down the best new restaurants and the finest vintages. On the right (yin) side, their knowledge of the better things in life is likely to have been taught to them by others – perhaps their parents have brought them up in a background of gentility and sophistication, or perhaps they have fallen in with a social circle that has educated them in such things.

The mark of sensuality applies to more than food – it also applies to sex. The subject is likely to be a connoisseur of sex as well, either a natural (yang) or an educated (yin) partner in bed. If they find themselves in the company of a sophisticated and experienced love, they will give their all, but faced with the amateurish fumblings of a virgin, they will not stay around for long.

The bearer of a mark of sensuality also risks overindulgence in many forms. If they are not too careful, they may become a glutton, of food, drink or sex. If they do not appear to be putting on weight, perhaps they are in search of ever stranger or more varied sexual practices to hold their jaded interests in the bedroom?

# The Mark of Diplomacy

A mole or birthmark on the outside corner of the chin can look at a first glance like a speck of dirt, a piece of stray food or a spot. This, according to face reading, is not necessarily a bad thing because it predisposes others against the subject, it can actually make them more active in forming friendships because they overcompensate. It can also make others find them somehow endearing, because they manage to appear unthreatening.

If the mark appears on the right (yin) side, the subject's life will be full of friends. No matter where they go, people find them instantly likeable and offers of help are never far away. The subject can remain perfectly passive and still have others seeking them out and offering their services.

If the mark appears on the left (yang) side, the subject will be far more likely to take an active interest in friendships. They have a natural gift in any social situation for putting people together, introducing perfect couples to each other and finding exactly the right sort of help at exactly the right time. These born diplomats have huge books of contacts and huge lists of favours they can call in, and if there is any problem at all with this feature, it is that they can simply be too popular and too busy. By virtue of their sheer usefulness, these diplomats will often attract hordes of toadies and hangers-on. There will always be people in life who are happy to be users of others' skills, but diplomats will attract much more than their fair share. Subjects who bear this particular mark are advised to stop regularly and take stock of the situation, and to ask themselves who their real friends are. Considering their skills, their real friends are likely to be the people who hang around them asking for favours the least often – and as people who like them for who they are, not what they can do, this makes them valuable indeed.

# Freckles and Spots

Moles and birthmarks are normally permanent, but other features of the face are much more transient. Freckles can come and go, and cold sores might recur regularly, but can be eliminated over time. The most temporary of all are spots, pimples and black-heads.

If a subject freckles easily, or their freckles are permanent, it is a sign of a friendly, gregarious person. Some face reading manuals suggest that the freckles are a crowd on the face, and that the subject is so popular that they carry their crowd around with them.

The temporary appearance of a freckle in any of the sectors described above represents an event in that area of the subject's fate. Something the subject has just done, or is just about to do, is going to have a visible effect on their fortune. It might balance another mole, it might add an influence which, when taken in context, might upset the good or bad fortune of the entire face – we are already into a relatively complex area of face reading, and can now see that the smallest alteration in one part of the face can change the effects of everything else.

A freckle may well be a good influence – it does not do any harm, and it could well turn up in very fortunate areas of a subject's fate. Pimples and spots, however, can be irritating, and rarely represent an improvement in someone's fate. Medical science tells us that these phenomena are caused by blocked pores and impurities in the diet, and the attitude of face reading is not far removed. It states that if something causes a spot to appear, the likeliest cause is a stress upon the body's inner source of energy. Stress, worry or concern about a wrong decision or an upcoming responsibility will cause poisons to appear in the body, and these impurities can be forced out through the skin. They are likely to be forced out through the sector of the face that has caused the poison to appear in the first place, giving us clues about the nature of the stress or concern. This is why teenagers have such a predisposition towards acne – their fate is in a constant state of flux, and new twists and turns are influencing it with every passing day. A good or bad teacher, a good or bad day at work, or a chance decision can all exert incredible influences on a young person's life, because decisions made during the teen years can affect education and employment, and these in turn can alter the subject's entire fortune.

The same applies to cold sores, though the long-term recurrence of a cold sore is an indicator that the problem in the subject's fate is deep-set, and will require a lot of effort on their part – perhaps even a complete change of lifestyle.

# Laughter Lines

Often confused with crow's feet (as we saw when looking at the eyes), laughter lines in Chinese face reading are not those lines on the face caused by the crinkling of the eyes when the subject laughs. Instead, they are lines caused by the positioning of the mouth in a smile, the bell-shaped curves that frame the mouth on either side.

In face reading, these lines are thought to show the subject's chances of living a long life. Because this is not thought to be determined until they reach adulthood and start to make decisions that affect their own fate, there is no need to be concerned if such lines do not appear on a child at all.

On adults, however, an average, perfectly acceptable life-span of the standard threescore-years-and-ten is denoted by laughter lines that terminate at the same level of the mouth. If the lines reach further than the mouth, and keep heading downward towards the chin, it is a sign that the subject can expect to live to an advanced old age.

Most laughter lines are bell-shaped, and will flare outwards slightly at their base. If, however, they point inward instead, it is a sign that foretells loneliness in old age. If the lines actually curve inwards and meet at the edge of the mouth, it suggests that, while they will always have a wide circle of friends to keep them company, the chances of great riches are remote indeed.

## CASE STUDY

Your ageing mother-in-law has surprised you all by announcing that she does not want to spend the holiday season with you. She claims that she would rather go and see her widowed friend, and that they would have a much better time without getting in the way of you 'young things' and your celebrations. Your relief is considerable (she can be a handful, after all), but you and your spouse suspect that this could be a double bluff. Is she expecting you to talk her out of it, or has she genuinely found something better to do than get under your feet?

Using your face reading skills as a guide, you notice that your mother-in-law's pronounced laughter lines curve inwards and meet at the edge of her mouth – a sure sign of friendship in old age. So there is no reason why she should not have friends. You have never really bothered looking at her face before, but now that you are scrutinizing the photographs, you also notice that she has a diplomatic mole on the right side of her face. This is another sign of friendship, but also of someone who might be prepared to save face. You rack your brain trying to think of anything you might have said last year to insult her, but you come up blank.

Then you notice something else at the corner of her eyes – *two* pronounced crow's feet instead of the expected one. You call her and discreetly enquire as to the gender of her widowed companion. She shyly confesses that he is male...

# TO THE HAIRLINE AND BEYOND

*The other part of the face where lines are most likely to be prominent is the forehead.* Such lines are often referred to in the West as 'worry lines', but they are not necessarily unfavourable in face reading. A single horizontal line across the forehead represents a brain that has been exercising (through frowns and concentration) from an early age, and is generally regarded as a sign of early success through hard work. This is particularly fortunate in the middle or upper part of the forehead. If the line comes down low, it suggests an early success on which the subject may be tempted not to capitalize. Such people run the risk of resting on their laurels too early, and paying the price by watching their fortunes slip away.

## Double and triple lines

If the lines on the forehead are double instead of single, it is a sign of supreme concentration and thought, and hence an indicator of high intelligence. Triple lines are more likely to stem not from high intelligence, but from the subject spending a lot of time in a state of surprise. Like certain other parts of the face (e.g. permanently raised eyebrows, eyes that show a lot of white all round), triple forehead lines denote a subject whose luck is eyebrow-raisingly incredible, who always seems to fall on their feet. Occasionally, the nature of the surprises that beset them may not be so fortunate, and as with other 'surprise' elements of the face, this is likely to be because of the subject's inability to see peripheral factors in any situation. Generally, however, triple forehead lines are a very beneficial feature.

# Diagonal Forehead Lines

A rarer form of forehead line does not run horizontally, but diagonally. These oblique lines can normally be seen when the subject raises a single eyebrow – if they regularly have this expression, it is likely gradually to etch a groove in their forehead. Such diagonal lines usually signify trouble ahead in human relationships, normally because the subject is simply too demanding. Such a person is likely to be very successful because they are harshly critical of their own shortcomings, but this razor-sharp intellect can backfire when turned on others.

If the diagonal line occurs on the left-hand (yang) side, others are liable to think them snobbish and aloof, with a permanently raised eyebrow that suggests someone ever ready with a pithy comment or an icy put-down. The yang diagonal line predisposes the subject to be the first with the criticism, whether or not it is invited. They risk becoming unpopular simply through venturing unwanted opinions. Although they may mean well, they have an uncanny knack of hurting others with the blunt truth.

If the diagonal line occurs on the right-hand (yin) side, the subject's fortune is more passive in nature. They are the type to raise a quizzical eyebrow in disgust and keep on walking by any situation they find themselves in. Their own belief that most situations are beneath them is likely to affect their fortune in an adverse way – this is the kind of thinking that means they never get the big breaks in career or relationships, because their own prejudices have ensured that they are never in the right place at the right time.

# Hair

Although the hair is not strictly part of the face, a couple of its features are mentioned here. As with eyes, the nature of the Chinese race has meant that face reading places less importance on differences in colour than it does on texture. As with eyes, the deeper the colour, the greater the energy levels of the subject, but face reading is above the generalities and frivolities of assigning someone a personality based solely on the colour of the hair.

Hair, like teeth, is produced from the body, and its state at any given time is a good indicator of the subject's health at the time when the hair was being produced. It is also influenced by the subject's state of mind, not through anything so esoteric as mental energy, but through the simple fact that someone in a state of depression is less likely to care for their hair than someone preparing for a dinner party. Very fine, smooth hair is a sign of creativity and perhaps shyness – the subject's head are not well-insulated from the world, and the subjects themselves are also likely to be affected adversely by hostile forces.

Coarse, stiff or frizzy hair that snags on a comb is a sign of a subject who is equally stubborn and hard to manage in other areas of their life. Once they have decided on a certain course of action, they are unlikely to change their mind in a hurry – a dogged refusal to give in that can pay dividends in life, but only if the initial decision happens to be the correct one.

Lank or greasy hair is a sign that the subject is similarly lacking animation in their life. Whether it is through the lacklustre energy that creates the hair in the follicle, or through their own inattention to hygiene, the end result is the same – drab hair that announces their own disillusionment.

Thinning hair is a sign of worry and stress, or perhaps just hard work. The complete absence of hair, in the manner of a Buddhist monk, is an indicator of someone who has dedicated themselves to a cause, normally a career. It is a sign that the subject does not have the time to concern themselves with the niceties of hairdressing – there is simply too much work to be done, and if they do not do it nobody will.

## Overcompensation

One final part of face reading for hair involves the amount of effort someone has devoted to caring for their hair. Considering their role in life and the occasion at which you find them, are they putting too much or too little into their hair? What is it they are trying to hide? Or are they too busy to think properly about their looks – if so, is this a sign of someone with more important things on their mind, or a gauche philistine with no sense of the importance of the occasion? Such observations depend totally on the situation in which you find yourself, and although they are moving beyond the bounds of traditional face reading, they can nevertheless spur some useful thoughts to aid with reading the face itself.

## CASE STUDY

You have been left in the lurch by a departing manager and now you have to appoint someone quickly. You have two choices in your office – Miss A, a pretty blonde assistant with slightly wavy medium-length blonde hair, or Mr B, a male senior member of staff with neat, slightly lank, grey hair.

Obviously, a large proportion of this decision will rely on common sense, as it should, and face reading can only supply a set of extra options to consider. In this case, you should be asking yourself why Mr B has not made it further in the company. He is neat and tidy on the surface, but does not take quite as much care with his appearance as you would like. Face it, his time has passed – he should be the outgoing manager, but for some reason, the previous candidate was a better choice. Miss A, on the other hand, might appear blonde and bubbly, but she is also lucky and successful. She is the one you should throw in the deep end, because if everything works out, the job is hers permanently.

# 9 PRECISION READINGS

*This book covers all the areas of basic face reading, but more experienced consultants have even more detailed charts and rules to follow. Just as professional horoscopes can dissect someone's birthday down to the nearest second (not month) and the actual place of birth, a truly accurate face reading needs to incorporate all of the above, and then go further into the areas of precision reading. Although we do not have much space to treat every aspect of precision readings, we can at least include the main elements, to help you on your way to truly detailed readings.*

Although we have already pointed out a few areas of the face where particular marks may have a certain influence on the subject's fortune, there are two other ways of dividing the face. Unfortunately, this means that for certain points on the face there will be three possible, and perhaps, contradictory readings. However, you may find that all three apply simultaneously, or that the presence of a precision reading edges out a previous one of which you were unsure anyway.

## Palaces of Fortune

The first precision area is that of the Palaces of Fortune, which simply divides the face up into areas of influence. Different parts of the face rule different parts of the character – in fact, we have already dealt with some of the basic areas, such as wealth being ruled by the nose. Here, however, are the rest:

| | |
|---|---|
| EYES | Intelligence |
| Under the Eyes | Children |
| Outer Tips of Eyes | Marriage/Affairs |
| EARS | Potential/Career |
| NOSE | Wealth/Business Acumen |
| MOUTH | Personability/Sociability |
| EYEBROWS | Wisdom/Emotional State |
| FOREHEAD | Education |
| Left/Yang Forehead | Father and his family |
| Right/Yin Forehead | Mother and her family |
| Lower-left Forehead | Friends |
| Lower-right Forehead | Siblings |
| TEMPLES | Travel |
| CHEEKBONES | Leadership |
| JAWBONE | Fame |
| CHIN | Strength |
| LAUGH LINES | Longevity |
| HAIR | Energy |

# Facial Division by Year

The other way of dividing up the face assigns a portion of the subject's life to each part of their face. Assuming a standard lifespan, we can pin this down to particular periods by area of the face. This may appear contradictory, but is actually an important foundation of face reading. Strictly speaking, we ought to cover it early on, because, for example, the ears' association with childhood and with potential are, essentially, aspects of the same reading. It is something of a chicken-and-egg situation as to which came first, the areas of fortune or the areas of age, because advanced face reading manuals regard them as codependent and coexistent. Advanced manuals of face reading have a specific sector of the face for every single year of the subject's life, but in this beginner's guide, we have restricted ourselves to general areas:

## AGES

| | |
|---|---|
| 0–13 | ears |
| 14 | top-centre of forehead |
| 15–18 | upper forehead |
| 19–23 | widow's peaks |
| 24 | lower forehead |
| 27 | bit between eyebrows |
| 28–29 | temples |
| 30–33 | eyebrows |
| 34–39 | eyes |
| 40 | bridge of nose |
| 41–42 | side of nostrils |
| 43–44 | bridge to middle of nose |
| 45–46 | left and right cheeks |
| 47 | tip of nose |
| 48–49 | left and right nostrils |
| 51–54 | top lip |
| 56–57 | end of moustache/left and right dimples |
| 58+ | mouth and below |

## CASE STUDY

So, how does this all work in practice? If a subject gets a spot on the end of their nose, previously we would have said it had something to do with their financial fortune. Now what do we say? The Palaces of Fortune chart still gives Finance as the area of importance, but the age chart quite specifically says that the area ruled is the subject's 47th year. Which is correct?

Your ruling on this should be determined by other factors. How old is the subject? If they are 46 there is a fair chance that whatever decision they have recently made may affect their fortune in their 47th year. If, however, the subject is only 12, the chances are low that a decision made now will impact directly on their fate in 35 years time.

If in doubt, go with the basic readings and/or the Palaces of Fortune, and save the years for times when the other parts of the face reading don not seem to add up.

# 10 Basic Charts

The charts below summarize most of the factors covered in the rest of the book. Entries in italics are ones that are part of face reading, but which have been omitted from this book due to available space. Most of them should be self-explanatory.

## Face Facts: Ruling Elements

| | | |
|---|---|---|
| Reddish | Fire | Hot-tempered, flustered |
| Blue/Black | Water | Sensitive, intellectual |
| Greenish | Wood | Slow but sure |
| White/Pale | Metal | Focused, sharp |
| Yellow/Brown | Earth | Reliable, strong |

## Nose

| | |
|---|---|
| Large tip | Great wealth |
| Small tip | Low income |
| Wide, flaring nostrils | Extrovert, generous |
| Thin, pinched nostrils | Introvert, miserly |
| Really wide, flaring nostrils | Extravagant (even if poor) |
| Really small nostrils | Miserly (even if rich) |
| Straight | (norma) |
| Crooked | Unlucky, unreliable |
| Hooked/downturned | Shrewd, careful, smart |
| Snub/upturned | Tactless, boastful, simple |
| Uneven | Stubborn/opinionated |
| Thin | Vain, critical |

| | |
|---|---|
| Broad | Unassuming, moderate |
| *Red* | *Overindulgence* |
| High bridge | Fortune and ease of living |
| Low bridge | Adversity, lack of energy |

## Mouth

| | |
|---|---|
| Big | Extrovert/show-off |
| Little | Introvert/meek |
| Top lip sticks past bottom lip | Shy, unassertive |
| Bottom lip sticks past top lip | Petulant, selfish |
| Wet | Emotional, energetic |
| Dry | Lack of qi, lethargic |
| Straight /normal | Good fortune |
| Straight/thick lips | Long life |
| Straight/thin lips | Powerful career |
| Upturned/normal lips | Happiness |
| Upturned/thick lips | Party animal |
| Upturned/thin lips | Hardship |
| Downturned/normal lips | Worry |
| Downturned/thick lips | Hardship |
| Downturned/thin lips | Always hopeful |
| Rosy red colour | Good fortune |
| Long dent in top lip | Long life |
| Dent is V-shaped | Hardship in old age |
| Dent is (-shaped | Hardship in early years |
| Lots of teeth | Good fortune |
| Missing teeth | Accident-prone |
| Widely spaced teeth | Indecisive |
| White teeth | Lucky |
| Yellow teeth | Lethargic |
| Green teeth | Very ill |
| Cheesy grin/big teeth | Long life |
| Little teeth | Childish, selfish |
| Pointed, wolf teeth | Cunning |
| Flat, cow teeth | Complacent, gullible |
| Inward-pointing, shark teeth | Lonely, solitary |
| Protruding, goat teeth | Shrewd, energetic, gregarious |

## Ears

| | |
|---|---|
| Large | Good fortune and good heart |
| Small | Shy and mean-spirited |
| Ears stick out | Flighty, easygoing |
| Ears pinned back | Nervous, skittish |
| Level with brow (top) and nostril (bottom) | Normal |
| Tip above brow | Selfish but successful |
| Base below nostril | Success in later life |
| *Lighter colouring than face* | *Good fortune* |
| *Redder than face* | *Hot-tempered* |
| *Darker than face* | *Easily impressed* |
| *Flaky skin* | *Bad in relationships* |
| Outer Wheel fat | Spoilt |
| Outer Wheel thin | Shrewd and cunning |
| *Pointed, elfin ear* | *Spiritual* |
| Inner Wheel sticks out | Outgoing, extrovert |
| Inner Wheel is flattened | Shy, introvert |
| Large ear hole | Open-minded |
| Small ear hole | Closed-minded |
| Long lobe | Long life and wisdom |
| Lobe attached to side of head | Possibly selfish |
| Hairy ears | Deaf to criticism |

## Eyes

| | |
|---|---|
| Blue | Happy, bright |
| Green/Olive | Magical, intelligent |
| Brown | Strong, energetic |
| Grey/Changeable | Fickle, unpredictable |
| Whites are very white | Powerful, energetic |
| Whites have bluish tint | Intuitive, magical |
| Whites are veiny | Overindulgence |
| Whites are yellowy | Low vitality |
| White shows beneath iris | Easily angered |
| White shows above iris | Snooty, hard to please |

| | |
|---|---|
| White shows all round | Possible ill health |
| Very large | Childlike, gullible |
| Round and large | Artistic, outgoing |
| Small | Shy, intense, complacent, secretive |
| Almond-shaped | Possibly vain |
| Almond-shaped and slanting up | Shrewd |
| Almond-shaped and slanting down | Confused, gullible |
| Deep-set | Intellectual, slow-starter |
| Protruding | Chancer, schmoozer |
| Triangular | Permanently perplexed |
| Rectangular | Philosophical |
| Half-moons | Cunning as a fox |
| Crossed eyes | Exacting, stressed |
| Eyes are close together | Stingy |
| Eyes are far apart | Charitable |
| Long lashes | Gentle, kind-hearted |
| Short lashes | Strong, aggressive |
| Heavy eyelids | Slow, complacent |
| Large lower lids | Sly, cunning |
| Crow's feet (left) | Number of spouses |
| Crow's feet (right) | Number of affairs |
| Tear tracks (left) | Misfortune through action |
| Tear tracks (right) | Misfortune through inaction |

## Brows

| | |
|---|---|
| Thick | Generous, fortunate |
| Thin | Snooty, unhelpful |
| Close together | Intense |
| Joined | Bad tempered, hypersensitive |
| Pointed and curved (Moon) | Emotional, clever |
| Blunt and curved (Lion) | Lucky, good-hearted |
| Thin and slightly curved (Delicate) | Beautiful, refined |
| Straight and horizontal (Number One) | Good organizer |

| | |
|---|---|
| Straight and pointing up in the middle (Number Eight) | Hassled, frustrated |
| Straight and pointing down in the middle (Dragon) | Fortunate, heroic |
| Thicker in the middle (Tiger) | Powerful, fierce |
| Gappy (Broken) | Bitter, badly treated |
| Chaotic | Disorganized |
| Curly | Egotistical, proud |
| Low | Intense, interfering |
| High | Eternally surprised |
| Thicker on the outside, pointed on the inside | Early marriage |
| Inner ends go vertical | Tough childhood |
| One higher than the other | Supercilious |
| Single line between | Ambitious, practical |
| Double line between | Artistic, hot-headed |
| Heavy brow bone | Fame |

## Cheekbones

| | |
|---|---|
| High and distinctive | Commanding |
| Narrow | Narrow-minded |
| Flat | Easy-going |
| Unbalanced | Very easy-going, shy, lazy |

## Jaw

| | |
|---|---|
| Broad yet rounded | Good fortune |
| Broad and square | Proud, stubborn, hard-working |
| Broad but broader at the ears | Hard, dominant |
| Round and smooth | Nothing to prove, content |
| Pointed | Early success without effort, vain |
| Very pointed | Never quite reaches their goals |

## Chin

| | |
|---|---|
| Square | Bold, brave, impulsive |
| Pointed | Blinkered, indecisive |
| Long and pointed | Interfering, gossipy |
| Round | Diplomatic |
| Protruding | Rash, pugnacious |
| Receding | Easily discouraged |
| Double chin | Lazy, unsporty |

## Hair

| | |
|---|---|
| Dark | High qi levels, energetic |
| Light | Low qi levels, lethargic |
| Blonde | Fun-loving |
| Red | Magical, hot-tempered |
| Brown | Keeps up with the times |
| Grey | Distinguished, mature |
| Grey (when young) | Tired, hardworking |
| Mousy | Indecisive |
| Two-tone | Sorcerer |
| Long (on men) | Rebellious |
| Very long (on women) | Idleness (risk of vanity) |
| Short (on women) | Efficient |
| Very short (on men) | Military, bold |
| Fine | Creative, shy |
| Thin | Worried, stressed out |
| No hair | Worried, stressed, venerable |
| Drab, flat | Unassertive |
| Bouncy | Lucky, easygoing |
| Curly | Tough, resilient |
| Very curly | Vain, self-regarding |
| Straight | Good heart |
| Wild | Wild person |
| Neat | Neat person |
| Coarse, frizzy | Forceful, stubborn |
| Beard or moustache | Wisdom |
| Bushy beard | Hiding something |

## Moles

| | |
|---|---|
| At top of forehead | Frustration |
| In middle of forehead | Success without love |
| Outside outer tip of eyebrow/temple | Travel (like it or not) |
| Between eyebrows | Great success |
| | Left: through charisma |
| | Right: through foresight |
| Weeping mole (below eye) | Miserable love life |
| | Left: own fault |
| | Right: someone else's fault |
| On upper cheek | Power without friendship |
| | Left: power hungry |
| | Right: unwilling leader |
| On lower cheek | Friends without family |
| | Left: overly sociable |
| | Right: unhappy family environment |
| On end of nose | Children/prosperity |
| | Left: through business acumen |
| | Right: inheritance |
| | Tip: spendthrift |
| On ears | Success without career |
| | Left: through own action |
| | Right: through luck |
| On outside upper lip | Gourmet or glutton |
| | Left: developed own love for food |
| | Right: inherited taste |
| On outside corner of chin | Diplomat, survivor |
| | Left: brings people together |
| | Right: makes friends easily |
| Freckles | Friendly/flirty |

## Lines in forehead

| | |
|---|---|
| Horizontal forehead line | Success |
| Horizontal forehead line (low down) | Limit to success (check left/right) |
| Two horizontal forehead lines | Potential genius |
| Three horizontal forehead lines | Extreme good luck |
| Oblique line to the left | Yang limitations |
| Oblique line to the right | Yin limitations |

## Laughter lines

| | |
|---|---|
| Slightly curved | Average |
| Bell-shaped, below mouth | Very long life |
| Long but curved in | Long life but lonely old age |
| Curve into mouth | Long life but poverty |
| Single vertical line | Stress and obstacles |
| Vertical lines between brows (two) | Good fortune |
| Vertical lines between brows (three) | Very good fortune |
| Vertical lines between brows (more than three) | Too many troubles |

# FURTHER READING

Chi An Kuei, *The Secret Language of Your Face*, Souvenir, 1998

Lip, Evelyn, *The Chinese Art of Face Reading*, Times Books International, 1989

Shen, Peter and Joyce Wilson, *Face Fortunes: The Ancient Chinese Art of Feature Reading*, Pelanduk Publications, 1990

Wu Ying, *Face Reading: Can you face the facts?*, Element, 1998